Pointe du Hoc

Pointe du Hoc

PETER HOWARD

Ian Allan
PUBLISHING

Acknowledgements:
The author wishes to thank the following:
John Ambler of the Royal Marines Museum, Gosport, Portsmouth, Hampshire.
Mons Chazette, Libraire Historie Fortifications, Paris, France.
Stephen Courtenay of the Royal Naval Museum, Portsmouth, Hampshire.
Emma Crocker and Chris Plant of the photograph archive at the Imperial War Museum, London.
Margaret Flott of the American Battle Monuments Commission, Arlington, Virignia, USA, and the staff at the American Cemetery at Colville-St. Laurent and the Pointe du Hoc Visitors Centre.
Denis Muir, the Clan Cameron Museum at Achnacarry Castle.
Richard Samways of the Weymouth Museum, Dorset.
Graham Thompson and Doug McCarthy of the National Maritime Museum, Greenwich, London.
Stephen Walton of the Imperial War Museum, Duxford, Cambridgeshire.

Further reading:
AMBROSE, Stephen E. *D-DAY. June 6 1944. The Battle for the Normandy Beaches.* (Pocket Books, 2002).
BOWMAN, Martin W. *Remembering D-Day: Personal Histories of Everyday Heroes.* (HarperCollins in association with the Imperial War Museum, London, 1994).
CHANDLER, David G. and COLLINS, James Lawton, Jr. (eds.) *The D-Day Encyclopaedia.* (Helicon, Oxford, 1994).
DARBY, William O. with Baumer, William H. *Darby's Rangers - We Led The Way.* (Ballantine Books, New York, 1993).
DILLON, Katherine V, GOLDSTEIN, Donald M., WENGER, J. Michael. *D-Day Normandy: The Story and Photographs.* (Brassey's (US) Washington 1994).
DOUGHTY, Martin (Ed.). *Hampshire and D-Day.* (Hampshire Books in association with Southgate Publishers, Crediton, 1994)..
DURNFORD-SLATER, Brigadier John. *Commando.* (William Kimber, London, 1953).
HASTINGS, Max. *Overlord. D-Day and the Battle for Normandy.* (Pan, London 1999).
HOGAN, David W. *U.S. Army Special Operations in World War II.* (University Press of the Pacific, 2004)
KILVERT-JONES, Tim. *Omaha Beach. V Corps Battle for the Normandy Beachead.* (Leo Cooper, Barnsley, 1999).
MAN, John. *Atlas of D-Day and the Normandy Campaign.* (Penguin, London, 1994)
REYNOLDS, David. *Rich Relations: The American Occupation of Britain 1942-45.* (HarperCollins, London, 1995)
RYAN, Cornelius. *The Longest Day.* (New English Library, London, 1969)
THOMPSON, Julian. *The Royal Marines. From Sea Soldiers to a Special Force.* (Sidgwick & Jackson, London, 2000).
WESTWELL, Ian. *US Rangers 'Leading the Way'.* (Ian Allan, Hersham, Surrey, 2003)

TITLE SPREAD: Douglas A-20B Havoc medium bombers return to base after bombing Pointe du Hoc. *(AN)*

Series Created & Edited by Jasper Spencer-Smith.
Design and artwork: Nigel Pell.
Produced by JSS Publishing Limited,
PO. Box 6031, Bournemouth, Dorset, England.

First published 2006

ISBN (10)0 7110 3095 2
ISBN (13) 978 0 7110 3095 4

Published by Ian Allan Publishing

an imprint of Ian Allan Publishing Ltd,
Hersham, Surrey KT12 4RG.
Printed by Ian Allan Printing Ltd,
Hersham, Surrey KT12 4RG.

Code: 0610/B

Visit the Ian Allan Publishing website at
www.ianallanpublishing.com

Photograph Credits
Clan Cameron Museum (CCM)
Imperial War Museum (IWM),
Libraire Historie Fortifications (LHF),
National Maritime Museum (NMM),
Royal Marines Museum (RMM),
Royal Navy Museum (RNM),
US Navy (USN),
Weymouth Museum (WyM).

CONTENTS

INTRODUCTION

'Will you tell me how we did this? Anybody would be a fool to try this. It was crazy then, and it's crazy now' – Lieutenant-Colonel James A Rudder, United States Army, revisiting Pointe du Hoc 10 years after he and his men had stormed the heights on D-Day.

Rudder was looking at the moonlike craters and shattered concrete bunkers and casements on top of cliffs 100ft (30.48m) high at Pointe du Hoc, lying between the beaches of Utah and Omaha on D-Day, 6 June 1944. Accompanied in 1954 by his 14-year-old son Bud and W. C. Heinz, a *Collier's* journalist, Rudder had good reason to question how Companies D, E and F of the 2nd Ranger Battalion, led by their colonel on the assault on the cliff, had managed such an incredible feat of arms.

In terms of casualties, it was a costly operation, and when the men who did reach the top unhurt discovered there was no sign of the expected 155mm guns in the casements, they must have questioned why. The Germans had moved them but the Rangers eventually did find them - and a large stockpile of ammunition - and destroyed the guns that could have caused havoc on both the beaches being invaded by their fellow Americans. But that was not the end of hard fighting because the Germans, having failed to defend Pointe du Hoc, reacted violently and did their utmost to eject the elite troops they were facing.

The Rangers held their ground, despite enemy attempts to prevent relieving forces reaching them. Yet after one day of fierce combat the three companies that comprised Ranger Force A had just 90 men capable of using weapons - from a total of 225 men who had begun to scale the cliffs. Their ascent, despite being fired on and suffering grenade attacks, was followed by determined defence of their newly won position. Their actions were truly heroic.

The 30-acre (12.14 hectares) battleground was pounded for some time before D-Day by Allied bombers, then warships supporting the infantry assault unleashed naval gunfire support shells onto the position. The area was hit by about 10 kilotons of explosive, approximately the power of the first atomic bomb dropped on the city of Hiroshima, 6 August 1945.

The remains of the bunkers and casemates are today much as they were after D-Day. Some are topped with viewing platforms for the benefit of visitors who range from veterans who fought at Pointe du Hoc and US Army cadets from West Point searching for knowledge, to holidaymakers, parties of schoolchildren and tourists with battlefield tours. Grass has softened some of the ravages of war but visitors still, like Col. Rudder, wonder how the Rangers did what they did.

RIGHT: Rangers undergoing training at a base in the USA. Recognition shoulder badges have been blanked out by the censor. *(JSS)*

US President Franklin D. Roosevelt did not like the word commando and wanted a name that had a more American ring to it – hence the choice of Rangers.

THE RANGERS

The formation by the United States Army of the Ranger battalions in World War Two can be traced to Winston Churchill. The Prime Minister of the United Kingdom of Great Britain and Northern Ireland, relieved as he was with the successful evacuation of so many British and Allied soldiers from the beaches of Dunkirk in 1940, knew that wars are not won with withdrawals. On 6 June 1940 - ironically four years to the day before D-Day - he sent a minute to General Lord Ismay, head of the Military Wing of the War Cabinet Secretariat, with various suggestions for making the lives of German soldiers difficult in their newly conquered territories. "Enterprises must be prepared", Churchill wrote, "with specially trained troops of the hunter class, who can develop a reign of terror down these coasts…" Action soon followed and from what Churchill envisaged as 'striking companies' emerged the soon to become familiar Commandos. (This word of Portuguese origin was taken from the original units formed by the Boers who gave the British Army such a difficult time in South Africa at the beginning of the 20th Century.) In January

LEFT: Members of the 3rd Rangers Battalion about to embark on Landing Craft Infantry (LCI) for the landings at Anzio, Italy, 22 January 1944. *(AN)*

1942, and a few weeks after Pearl Harbor, United States President Franklin D. Roosevelt ordered the formation of American commando-style units.

However, the President did not like the name associated with the British Army's elite units - and required something with a more American 'ring' to it. So the Rangers of the 20th Century were born.

As the United States Army's *Lineage Series: Infantry Part I - Regular Army* (1972) states: "Rangers were a species of infantry that the British had developed to cope with the methods of the French and Indians in North America. They were scouts who ranged the forests spying upon the enemy, gathering intelligence on his strength and intentions, and harassing him when they could. Units of rangers had to be made up of men who understood wood-craft and who could match the Indians in stealth. Also, they had to be trained shots". One of the most famous Rangers, Robert Rogers, was born (1731) in Massachusetts, grew up in New England and became an American colonial army officer. He was already experienced in hunting and exploring.

By the end of the French and Indian War (1763) he was one of the best known military men in the colonies and as a major had commanded nine ranger companies. He was one of those men to whom war brought out the best, whereas peace had the reverse effect and he died in obscurity in London in 1795. His military feats and flair were sufficient for him to be remembered in World War Two when the rules he drew up for Rangers in 1757 were reprinted to inspire the new Rangers. One American historian, Fred Anderson, has claimed that Rogers was perhaps not as good a backwoodsman as he was a self-publicist.

There is strange irony in that the 18th century skills of an American colonial were of considerable assistance to a British Army drilled for rigid combat in lines and not for using initiative and woodcraft. Nearly two hundred years later, a fast-growing but still very small United States Army turned to British Army Commandos for initial training in the art of making life difficult for Germans. The Americans were fortunate, too, in that the man tasked with developing elite troops was Lucian King Truscott Jr., a temporary brigadier general who was attached to Lord Louis Mountbatten's British combined operations staff. Truscott, a real 'soldier's soldier', had also studied the British commando operations. He went on to replace the famous General George S. Patton in command of the US 3rd Army after the war. The man Truscott selected to lead the new 1st Ranger Battalion was Captain (Capt.) William O. Darby, a West Point graduate who called for volunteers from the US Army's 1st

ABOVE: Training at Achnacarry for British Commandos and US Rangers was made as 'realistic' as possible with the use of explosives and live gunfire. *(CCM)*

RIGHT: A British instructor demonstrates to a US Ranger the art of camouflaging a helmet. The rifle is a .303 Lee-Enfield which was the standard British infantry weapon. *(IWM)*

LEFT: Some of the first British soldiers to volunteer for training at the School for Unconventional Warfare, later renamed the Commando Basic Training Centre. *(IWM)*

LEFT: Fitness was a very important part of Commando training. One of the most favoured exercises was log tossing. *(IWM)*

RIGHT: British soldiers at Achnacarry training in assault from behind and the use of the dagger. *(IWM)*

RIGHT: Crossing a river by a ropeway. One of the many skills to be achieved by any soldier wishing to become a Commando. *(IWM)*

LEFT: The 'graves' at Achnacarry. When one US Ranger asked who was buried in one the reply was "a soldier who didn't clean his rifle". *(CCM)*

LEFT: Commandos training at Achnacarry. *(CCM)*

Armored Division and 34th Infantry Division and other units already training in Northern Ireland. As author David W. Hogan pointed out in his *U.S.Army Special Operations in World War II* the men came from all over the United States and included a former lion tamer and a full blooded Sioux Indian. They were formed into a headquarters company and six companies each 67 men strong.

Then came intensive training at Achnacarry Castle (seat of the Clan Cameron) north of Fort William in the west highlands of Scotland. Achnacarry is a name synonymous with commandos and 25,000 British Army, Royal Marines also men from Allied nations - French, Belgian, American, Dutch and Norwegian soldiers learned their basic commando skills there in the first three years of the war. Training was hard and physically very demanding. Apart from long and forced marches with heavy burdens, battle conditions were replicated as realistically as possible … with the firing of live ammunition.

Unarmed combat, weapons training, night operations, patrolling and getting used to small boats were all included. Soldiers who failed to meet the demanding standards of training, discipline and self-discipline were RTU'd. To the layman, that is Returned To Unit, or being sent back to their previous service unit. Some units sent some of their worst soldiers as volunteers - as an unbelievable chance to get rid of miscreants. Such men were soon found out by the commandos and rejected, though in a few rare cases it was discovered that some men unwanted by their own regiment or corps could meet commando expectations, provided they were given a second chance and the right leadership. It did not take long for the Rangers to follow the methods of their British hosts.

Above the village of Spean Bridge, close to Achnacarry, there is a Commando Memorial – three towering figures in battledress reminding visitors of the brave men who trained in tough conditions against the background of Britain's highest mountain, Ben Nevis 4,406 ft (1,343m). British commandos who, on qualification were entitled to wear the now much-coveted green beret, went on to win 38 battle honours and among many individual medals were eight Victoria Cross (VC), 37 Distinguished Service Order (DSO) and 218 Military Medal (MM). The original units, Nos 3 and 4 Commando, were formed from Army volunteers in 1940. The Royal Marines (RM) in November 1940 called for the first volunteers for 'hazardous duty' from the ranks. It is not surprising that some leaders in government did not like the adoption of the word 'Commando' because of the Boer War memories. They wanted 'Special Service' troops, until it was pointed out that the abbreviated form 'SS' (*Schutzstaffel*) was used by the Nazis' version of elite troops! Even so, Special Service Brigades was the title for some time until replaced in the last year of the war by Commando Brigades. Furious in opposition to 'SS' was Lieutenant-Colonel (Lt.-Col.) John Durnford-Slater, the man who raised the first Commando, No.3. As he recalled in his 1953 memoir, *Commando*, if he received a letter from the War Office in Whitehall addressed to him as 'Officer Commanding A Company, Special Service Battalion' he would reply as 'Officer Commanding No.3 Commando'. Looking back he thought he was being stubborn, even a bit schoolboyish but before many weeks "the War Office surrendered. We were No.3 Commando, and no-S.S. nonsense about it".

Durnford-Slater went on to command a brigade and earned a DSO and Bar. The number 3 was chosen for the first Commando because if intelligence should reach German ears, they could be deceived into thinking the British had more elite troops than was the case. Commissioned into the Royal Artillery, Durnford-Slater formed his commando into 10 troops of three officers and 47 men each. Including headquarters there were 35 officers and 500 men - and the British wanted nine more Army units of similar size. When the RM battalions were converted into Commandos in 1942, it meant a surplus of personnel because of the reduction from a normal infantry battalion to 500 and many of the officers and men were transferred to landing craft duty.

Maj. Darby was impressed with the training at Achnacarry and got on well with the Commanding Officer, Lt.-Col. Charles Edward Vaughan, once a Guards drill instructor.

US Rangers crossing a ditch filled with barbed wire on one of the many assault courses at Achnacarry. *(IWM)*

US Rangers crossing the Glasgow to Mallaig railway line under the cover of smoke grenades during training at Achnacarry Castle. (IWM)

Vaughan commanded what was initially the School for Unconventional Warfare, later the Commando Training Centre. In his co-authored *Darby's Rangers*, published years after his death, Darby wrote: "The British Commandos did all in their power to test us to find out what sort of men we were. Then, apparently liking us, they did all in their power to prepare us for battle". Training over, the commandos were deployed on a number of small-scale raids such as on Guernsey in the Channel Islands, and on the islands of Lofoten and Vaagso in Norway, but then came a much bigger operation - the assault on Dieppe (18-19 August 1942) on the French coast. This amphibious assault code-named Jubilee was bigger than a raid and involved 5,000 soldiers, mainly Canadian, of whom 3,400 became casualties. There were claims Dieppe was necessary in order to gain crucial lessons for what was to become later the greatest amphibious invasion force of all time …D-Day. This was a very painful way to learn a lesson and gave added ammunition to the critics who claimed the British have always been good at using Commonwealth troops in preference to their own. There is an alternative school of thought: that senior Canadian officers were desperate to prove the worth of their troops. Despite some acts of gallantry, and some learning, the result was a disaster and Americans were among the casualties. The new Rangers had provided 50 men for the Dieppe experience, attached to two British Army commandos tasked with silencing gun batteries on the flanks of the main operations. No 4 succeeded but the German Navy ensured that No 3 would not.

There were 'firsts' for the Rangers involved: two officers, Second Lieutenants (2/Lt.) Edward V. Loustalot and Joseph H. Randall were killed and so was Technician 4th Grade (T/4) Howard W. Henry. They were the first Americans to die facing Germans in combat after the USA entered the war. At this point, it should be remembered there were Americans who died before their nation took up arms against the Axis powers. They included fighter pilots running the risk of losing their citizenship because they were in breach of neutral power regulations, or seamen assisting convoys that provided vital lifelines for Britain

LEFT: Achnacarry Castle today. *(CCM)*

RIGHT: The location of Achnacarry Castle with Ben Nevis in the background. *(CCM)*

when the country was standing alone. One Ranger, Corporal (Cpl.) Franklin Koons, is on record as being the first US Army soldier to kill a German in combat in this war. The new Rangers had been 'blooded' and four officers and 39 men returned from Dieppe and were soon to head for another theatre of war - North Africa. With Darby's men gone, there was no US unit to help the British continue their raiding activities.

The 29th Ranger Battalion was formed from the 29th Infantry Division - a US National Guard formation with men from Virginia and Maryland. The volunteers trained for five weeks at Achnacarry and then joined their British comrades in raids on Norwegian and French coasts in 1943, on one of which the entire battalion took part in destroying a German radar post on the Ile d' Ouessant (Ushant) off north-west Brittany. Despite this, the outfit was deactivated on 15 October 1943. In the US Army there was opposition to the formation of further Rangers. Just as in other armies, special - or elite - troops were regarded by some senior officers as costly, a diversion from the business of 'serious' standard units who suffered when some of their more talented officers and senior non-commissioned officers volunteered for hazardous operations. This controversy exists today and historians seldom agree over the value of special units in World War Two. US Army Chief of Staff General (Gen.) George Catlett Marshall (1880-1959) overruled the dissenters and the 2nd Ranger Battalion came into being on 11 March 1943. The men were initially trained at Camp Forrest, Tennessee, under the command of Major (Maj.) L. E. McDonald but on 30 June, Maj. James Earl Rudder took over. New York, Pennsylvania and New Jersey were the states providing most of the men.

Intensive training at Camp Forrest was followed by more at Fort Pierce, Florida where assault craft and small boats were featured and then at Fort Dix, New Jersey, for advanced tactical preparation. Once deemed ready for active service 2nd Rangers left for England on 21 November 1943 on the liner RMS *Queen Elizabeth*, leaving behind the 5th Ranger Battalion, formed on 1 September at Camp Forrest, also going through training. They sailed for Europe in January 1944.

As the numbers of Commandos and Rangers grew, the parts of the world where their skills were required also became more numerous, but this story continues with special emphasis on the 2nd Ranger Battalion and to a lesser extent, the 5th Ranger Battalion.

The Ranger Creed

Recognizing that I volunteered as a Ranger, fully knowing the hazards of my chosen profession, I will always endeavor to uphold the prestige, honor, and high esprit de corps of my Ranger Regiment.

Acknowledging the fact that a Ranger is a more elite soldier who arrives at the cutting edge of battle by land, sea, or air, I accept the fact that as a Ranger my country expects me to move farther, faster and fight harder than any other soldier.

Never shall I fail my comrades. I will always keep myself mentally alert, physically strong and morally straight and I will shoulder more than my share of the task whatever it may be. One-hundred-percent and then some.

Gallantly will I show the world that I am a specially selected and well-trained soldier. My courtesy to superior officers, neatness of dress and care of equipment shall set the example for others to follow.

Energetically will I meet the enemies of my country. I shall defeat them on the field of battle for I am better trained and will fight with all my might. Surrender is not a Ranger word. I will never leave a fallen comrade to fall into the hands of the enemy and under no circumstances will I ever embarrass my country.

Readily will I display the intestinal fortitude required to fight on to the Ranger objective and complete the mission though I be the lone survivor.

RANGERS LEAD THE WAY!

The closest possible co-operation between government, business and the workforce in the US led to a prodigious industrial war effort.

2

ENGLAND AND D-DAY

By now, most people with just a modest knowledge of military history are aware of the basic planning of the D-Day operations. So are many people who may not be particularly interested in history at all - but have probably watched the film *The Longest Day* on one or more of the many times it has been shown on tv since it appeared in 1962, based on the book of the same title by Cornelius Ryan. The aim was to land approximately 175,000 troops by air or sea on the channel coast beaches of Normandy from a point in the west at the Carentan estuary to a point in the east near Ouistreham. Nearly 5,000 Allied ships and craft would be involved, and so would three divisions of airborne troops to secure the flanks of the seaward assault. That was the plan, the larger parts of which did not concern the 2nd and 5th Rangers, desperately keen to ensure that their part in this amazing day worked. Once battle is joined the soldier does not have time to think about the 'big picture' - just the one that is affecting himself and his comrades.

A Ranger aware of his immediate responsibilities was probably unaware of the sheer

LEFT: Three Landing Craft Assault (LCA) return to base on Loch Arkaig after an exercise. The loch is very close to Achnacarry Castle and the remote location made it ideal for the secret training of Commandos and US Rangers. *(CCM)*

scale of the US war effort. In an article to mark the 50th anniversary (June 1994) of D-Day, historian Stephen E. Ambrose wrote in *Army* magazine that US industry in 1939 had been severely depressed with unemployment over 20%. Government, industry and unions were constantly bickering, almost at war with one another. "It took the challenge of Nazism to bring unity of purpose and teamwork to America, but when it came, it was a prodigious force. What Gen. Dwight D. Eisenhower called 'the fury of an aroused democracy' led to the closest possible cooperation between government, business and labour. Between 1941 and 1944, factory capacity in the United States was not just fully utilized, it was doubled - and then doubled again - and then again. In 1939, the United States had produced 800 aircraft, less than half of them for the military - at a time when the *Luftwaffe* had 5,000 planes.

"When President Roosevelt called for the production of 4,000 airplanes per month, people thought he was crazy. By 1942, the United States was already producing 4,000 a month, and by the end of 1943, 8,000 per month. There were similar, all but unbelievable

A US Ranger on the 'rope slide' from the roof of Achnacarry Castle. *(CCM)*

Training in
house-to-house
combat at a
location in
Scotland. He is
carrying a .30
calibre M1
Garand semi-
automatic rifle
with bayonet.
(IWM)

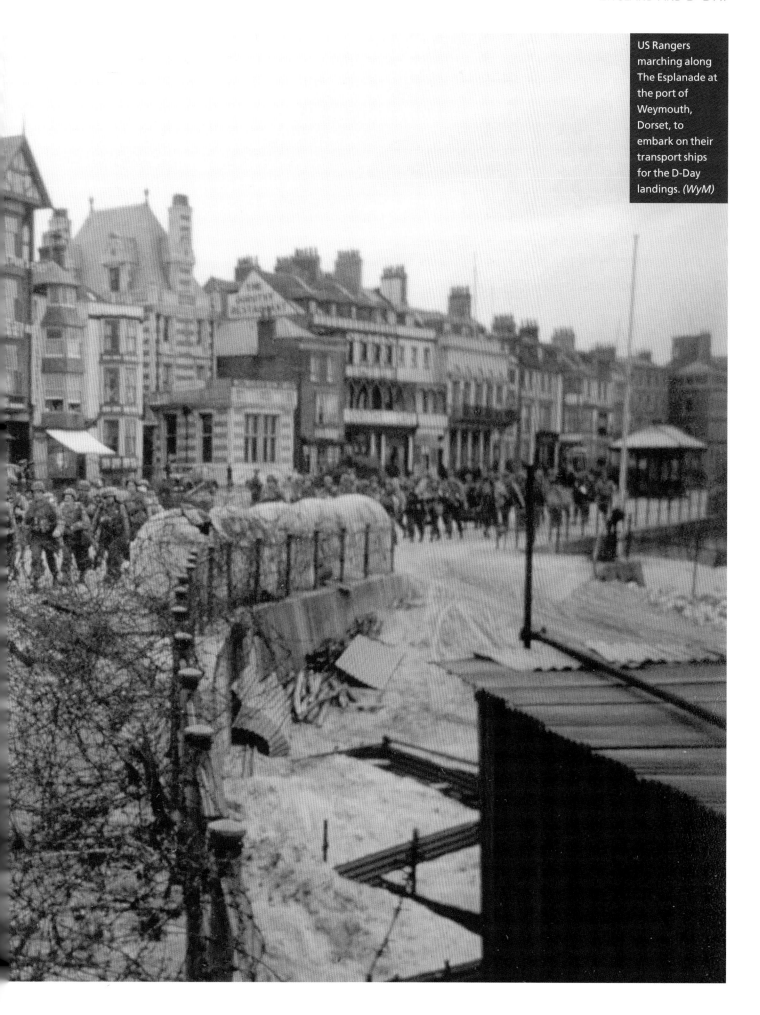

US Rangers marching along The Esplanade at the port of Weymouth, Dorset, to embark on their transport ships for the D-Day landings. *(WyM)*

great leaps forward in the production of tanks, ships, landing craft, rifles and other weapons."

Ambrose went on to point out that it was incredible what teamwork - voluntary team-work, brought about by a determined, outraged people could accomplish and not just in industrial production. In 1939, the US Army was 175,000 men strong. It ranked 16th in the world, right behind Romania. The writer went on to say the other 'miracle' of America in World War Two was the creation, almost from scratch, of a citizens' army that could challenge the Wehrmacht on the continent of Europe. ".... in the spring of 1944 whether those democratic armies could outfight the Nazis' armies remained to be seen. In looking at the contending sides on the eve of the invasion of France, the first thing that stands out is the trust and confidence that characterized the Allied High Command in contrast with the mistrust

and doubts that dominated the Nazi High Command".

Before they could face the Germans, the Rangers had to get used to the United Kingdom, where in the view of David Reynolds in his book *Rich Relations: The American Occupation of Britain 1942-45* (1995), American servicemen: "Compared with the British (let alone the French or Germans) they were better paid and better fed. Their wealth could cut through the class barriers of the Old World enabling them to buy a meal at London's best restaurants where no English private would get past the doorman." The 2nd Ranger Battalion continued amphibious training in Scotland at HMS *Dorlin*, a large country house (once the seat of Clanranald) at Acharacle, a village at the head of Loch Shiel in the west highlands of Scotland. The house was commissioned into service on 23 March 1942

ABOVE: A pre-D-Day exercise probably at Bude, Cornwall. A rocket grapnel has been fired whilst a Medic attends to a 'casualty'. Note the lightweight tubular-steel ladders. *(JSS)*

ABOVE: The helmsman and gunner's position on a Landing Craft Assault (LCA). *(WyM)*

and decommissioned on 28 November 1944 and was later demolished. Other locations included Bude, Cornwall, Woolacombe, North Devon and Warsash, Hampshire, a county where the well-known Needles on the Isle of Wight and accompanying cliffs provided ideal assault training. Warsash on Southampton Water was also home to other special units - though the local civilians probably did not know this at the time. These included hydrographic surveyors, swimmers and others who gathered crucial information regarding the beaches and the obstacles facing any D-Day invaders. It was at Warsash where 22-year-old Sergeant (Sgt) Owen L. Brown of HQ Company, 2nd Rangers discovered that not all the natives were friendly. Russell Miller included in *Nothing Less Than Victory. The Oral History of D-Day* (1993) the following recollection of Sgt. Brown: "When we arrived at Warsash, Mrs Downs, the wife of a

British Army general serving in India, said she had room for eight Yanks. We were greeted at the door by the maid.

"As the last Yank walked in, the maid reached down, picked up her bag, and left. She refused to work for any damn Yankees. The lady of the house did all the cooking and cleaning while we were there.

"The house we were in had 1594 chiselled in the fireplace mantel, and it is still a very solid structure to this day. It was constructed by putting up a framework of hand-hewn timbers and my bed was in the roof area, between crossbeams holding the sides together. When I tried to get up in a hurry, I would hit my head on a beam. This was a particular danger after spending a few hours at the local pub, when beer made me run for the bathroom in a hurry. The bathroom was on the second floor landing, so I had further to go than the rest of them.

"Mrs Downs had purchased the home right after their home in London had been bombed. The only people she knew in Warsash was the butcher. With the strict rationing the English had, it was hard to get meat. Mrs Downs came home with many parcels labelled `rabbit' or `chicken' that contained mutton. We actually sat around the table in the dining room as a family. Her favourite dish was mutton roasted with quarter potatoes cooked in the meat around it and served with brussel sprouts.

We did learn to enjoy this, as it made a change from our GI mess hall".

If nothing else, this evidence confirms the view of David Reynolds that in the British Isles all Americans were viewed as 'Yanks', whichever state they came from. He thought many GIs came to accept the view "they were all Yanks - overseas, the similarities outweighed the differences".

There happened to be a lot of such men in the UK. On 30 April 1944 there were over 1,442,000 of them. Wiltshire hosted 136,340, Hampshire 86,482, Devon 85,191 and Suffolk 71,105. The most 'American' county in the north was Lancashire, with 63,469 - possibly as a result of Liverpool being a point of disembarkation. As D-Day neared the populations of the southern and south-west counties rose still further because of the movements south of units to embark for Operation Overlord.

For two men of this huge visiting army, Rudder and the commanding officer of the 5th Ranger Battalion, Maj. Max F. Schneider, January 1944 was crucial because in that month they had to visit the operations officer of Lieutenant-

ABOVE: HMS *Prince Charles*, built in 1934 as a short-sea crossing (Ostende-Dover) passenger ferry operated by the Belgium government. The ship was converted to carry Landing Craft Assault (LCA) which transported the Rangers to Pointe du Hoc. The vessel was returned to passenger service after the war. (IWM)

General (Lt.-Gen.) Omar N. Bradley's First (US) Army, Colonel (Col.) Truman Thorson.

It was then they learned of their mission - Pointe du Hoc (Author David W. Hogan, Jr., refers to Pointe du Hoe [sic] and in this he is not alone. Numerous official accounts and some historians contain the same mis-spelling. Mind you, errors in the spelling of Scottish locations have been found by this writer in official RN documents). One intelligence officer, belonging to the staff of Rear-Admiral (R-Adm.) John L. Hall, USN, is reported to have said the task facing the Rangers was impossible and that three old women with brooms could sweep the Rangers off the cliff. The Rangers officers were said by Hogan to be 'stunned' by the magnitude of the task - but then stepped up the cliff-climbing techniques and amphibious training.

Planning in some form for a return to the European mainland had never been far from Churchill's mind since Dunkirk. Yet it was in April 1943, well before the choice of a Supreme Commander, that British Lt.-Gen. Frederick Morgan was appointed Chief of Staff to the Supreme Allied Commander (COSSAC). There was a lot of planning to be done but among the detail was what, to some, seemed a simple issue: an infantry assault was the only certain way to silence the six 155mm guns believed to be at Pointe du Hoc. And the Rangers had been formed with very difficult tasks in mind! The guns that commanded both Utah and Omaha beaches could also bombard the vast number of naval targets. These guns had to be put out of action. On 5 May 1944, the two Ranger battalions joined together at Dorchester,

Dorset in southern England. On 9 May the newly named Provisional Ranger Group learned that Lt.-Col. Rudder would be in command. The plan for D-Day saw the Rangers temporarily attached to the 116th Infantry Regiment of the 29th Infantry Division and the Rangers were split into three groups:

Task Force A - comprised 2nd Ranger Battalion's Companies D, E and F, along with elements of Headquarters Company. To them fell the daunting task of destroying the 155mm guns believed to be located at Pointe du Hoc. Task Force A were transported by personnel ships (ex-Channel and Irish Sea ferries with the hand-operated davits) serving as Landing Ships Infantry (Hand), SS *Ben-My-Chree* (Company E, Company F, and HQ) and SS *Amsterdam* (Company D and Company E) and were to land at Pointe du Hoc at 0630. SS *Ben-My-Chree* had been damaged during the evacuation of troops on the beaches of Dunkirk – so a return journey to France for the crew as part of an attack must have been welcome.

Task Force B was Company C of the 2nd Ranger Battalion supported by a platoon of Duplex Drive (DD) tanks from Company B of the 743rd Tank Battalion. These units were to land at Charlie Sector (adjacent to Dog Green Sector) near Company A of the 116th Infantry Regiment of the 29th Infantry Division. This force had two plans, the first to follow Company A through this assault on Vierville and on to a German strongpoint at Pointe Raz de la Percée, and the second to directly attack the point via

ABOVE: SS *Empire Javelin* originally named SS *Cape Lobos* launched in 1944 for service with the US War Shipping Administration. The vessel was bareboat chartered by the Transport Department of the British Ministry of War and managed by the Blue Star Line. She was sunk by U-772 on 28 December, 1944. *(NMM)*

cliffs if Vierville was not cleared. Once Pointe Raz de la Percee was cleared they were to link up with the Rangers of Task Force A at Pointe du Hoc. The Ranger units of Task Force B were transported by the Landing Ship Infantry (Small), (LSI[S]) HMS *Prince Charles*, and rendezvoused with Company A units of the 116th Infantry Regiment transported in the Landing Ship Infantry (Large), (LSI[L]) SS *Empire Javelin* before making their run to Omaha Beach. Company C was to land at 0633.

Task Force C was made up of the 5th Ranger Battalion and Companies A and B of the 2nd Ranger Battalion. This force was to wait offshore until 0700 when a pre-arranged signal from Task Force A told them to either: land at Pointe du Hoc and assist Task Force A, or land at Omaha Beach and proceed through the Vierville draw and on to Pointe du Hoc. The units of Task Force C were transported by LSI(L)s HMS *Prince Charles* (Company A, Company B and 5th Rangers), HMS *Prince Leopold* (5th Rangers) and HMS *Prince Baudouin* (5th Rangers).

In common with the vast majority of the Allied men due to land on the beaches, the Rangers were well trained, well motivated and determined to prove their worth. They were also, with a few exceptions, newcomers to battle compared to hardened units like the US Army's 1st Infantry Division (Big Red One) and the British 51st Infantry Division (Highland). The plans being well laid, and the men now as ready as could possibly be, 2nd and 5th Ranger Battalions just waited for the day.

'The Garand was a big advance on any rifle we had handled in the Commandos'. This was a senior British officer's tribute to the Rangers' M1

3

THE ATTACKERS

The year 1942 saw the .30 calibre Garand M1 semi-automatic replacing the Springfield M1903A1 bolt-action rifle that US troops had arrived in the UK with, though some (M1903A4) were retained for sniping purposes until the early 1960s. The Garand certainly appealed to the British troops who had a chance to fire the weapon. Some had the chance to obtain one - including the man, already mentioned, who raised the first British Army Commandos: Lt.-Col. John Durnford-Slater. When the Rangers 20-strong party arrived to join No.3 Commando in preparation

for the Dieppe assault, their leader Capt. Roy Murray offered the British chance to try the rifle on the range. Then, to Durnford-Slater's delight, the American gave it to him, and there were a few more for troop commanders. The British officer recalled: "I found the weapon accurate, easy to handle, quick, and generous with firepower: much better than the short-range Tommy gun (Thompson sub-machinegun) I had been using. Without a doubt the Garand was a big advance on any rifle we had yet handled in the Commandos". Officers were often issued with the carbine

LEFT: The .30 calibre M1 Garand semi-automatic rifle was standard issue to the Rangers and was probably the best infantry rifle of World War Two. *(JSS)*

LEFT: The .30 calibre M198A2 Browning Automatic Rifle (BAR) had a 20-round box magazine. *(JSS)*

RIGHT: US forces including the Rangers underwent many training exercises in preparation for the D-Day landings on 6 June 1944. *(JSS)*

RIGHT: The famous .45 calibre M1911 Colt automatic pistol. This weapon was standard US issue from World War One until the 1980s. *(JSS)*

version, which could take a magazine of 15 or 30 rounds compared with the standard ammunition clip of eight rounds. The rifle became popular with other nations, too, and in his *D-Day* book Stephen Ambrose points out that later in 1944 German troops could also be found using some captured M1s. Over six million Garands were made from 1936 to 1959.

Sub-machineguns were quickly accepted as effective in this war and Rangers were equipped with the Thompson M1928, adopted for service use initially by the United States

RIGHT: The .45 calibre M1A1 Thompson sub-machine gun (SMG) was nicknamed 'The Gangster Gun' by British forces. *(JSS)*

RIGHT: The .45 calibre M3A1 sub-machine gun became the US Army's standard issue SMG. The weapon was given the name 'Grease Gun' by troops. *(JSS)*

LEFT: US troops relax aboard the transport which will take them to the beaches. *(WyM)*

ABOVE: US
Rangers about to
embark on an LCA
and be taken out
to a Landing Ship
(Infantry). One
Ranger is equipped
with a 'Bangalore
Torpedo', an
explosive weapon
used to break
through barbed-
wire defences.
(WyM)

Marine Corps as the Thompson M1. The weapon was disliked by some servicemen because of use by gangsters, but it was extremely useful. The .45 cartridge could be in magazines of 20 or 30 rounds - or drum containing either 50 or 100 rounds. Former Jane's weapons specialist the late Ian Hogg claimed that for reliability and construction, few guns "have ever come close to the Thompson". Also using a .45 cartridge - though it could be adapted to take 9mm ammunition - was the lighter M3 'grease gun', lighter than the Thompson and though manufactured in its thousands was only in production for two years, 1942 to 1944.

Most officers carried the .45 Colt M1911 pistol, a weapon that saw service - with the follow on M1911A1 - from 1911 to 1990. It was the smallest firearm carried and being

a lightly armed force, the heaviest weapons carried by the assault troops were the Browning Automatic Rifle (BAR) with four allocated to each company. The BAR fired a .30 cartridge, with 20 rounds in a box magazine. Each company also had two 60mm mortars, a weapon that could fire a 3lb (1.36 kg) bomb nearly 2,000 yds (1,829m) and was fitted with a proper sighting mechanism.

The Rangers also had British-style Commando knives, US Army standard issue bayonets and hand grenades - the M1 grenade was actually a French design adopted by the US Army in 1917. The design might have been old, but the contents had become more varied. White phosphorous for smoke, blast for stunning the enemy and thermite (more of this later) were some of the varieties.

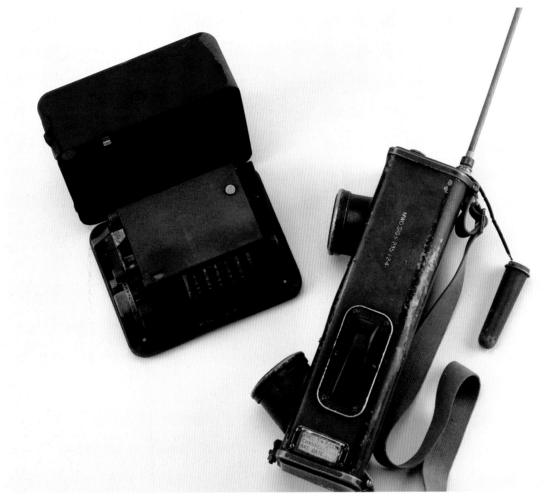

LEFT: US Army standard issue 'Walkie-Talkie' radio. *(JSS)*

BELOW: The .30 calibre M1919A4 Browning light machine gun mounted on the standard M2 tripod. The air-cooled gun was a very reliable weapon. *(JSS)*

What with the weapons, helmets and combat clothing there was little to distinguish the Rangers from any other unit heading for Omaha beach... apart from some very distinctive equipment to use in cliff climbing. The most spectacular items were four 100ft (30.5m) extension ladders, supplied by the London Fire Brigade, mounted on DUKWs (D: 1942 version. U: amphibian. K: all-wheel-drive. W: twin-rear axles). Rudder had sent two of his best men, Staff Sergeant (S/Sgt.) Jack Kuhn and Private First Class (PFC) Peter Karpalo, to work with the fire appliance manufacturer Merryweather in London to solve the problem of getting men to the top of Pointe du Hoc in the most effective way. Two machine guns mounted on the top of such ladders would help to keep German heads down while Rangers climbed the cliffs in a more pedestrian manner. Each of 10 Landing Craft Assault (LCA) to take Rangers to the beaches was equipped with rocket guns to fire grapnels, pulling 3/4 in (19mm) plain ropes, toggle ropes and rope ladders. Tubular steel extension

Four DUKW vehicles were fitted with a 82ft (25m) London Fire Brigade extending ladder mounted with two aircraft-type .303 Lewis guns. One DUKW was sunk on the approach to the shore. The three remaining reached the beach but could not get close to the cliff due to the loose shingle and wet clay on the landing site. Only one ladder was extended. *(RMM)*

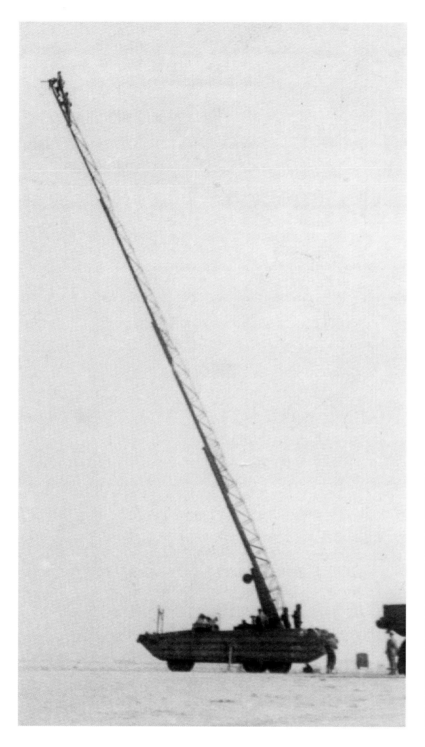

ABOVE: A DUKW on trials with the ladder fully extended. *(RMM)*

ABOVE RIGHT: On a training excercise, probably at Bude, Cornwall, with Rangers climbing the ladder. *(JSS)*

ladders in light, four-foot sections for speedy assembly were also carried in the LCAs. The Rangers would be moving 'light' and two supply craft were to follow carrying personal equipment, extra ammunition, rations and demolition charges for the three companies making for Pointe du Hoc.

A blue diamond was the 2nd Ranger insignia, and was worn into battle on D-Day, even though it was not popular with the soldiers because it resembled a commercial logo. The shoulder title - 2D RANGER BN- was not worn. By late 1944. the 2nd Rangers began wearing a different design based on the one previously worn by the 1st, 3rd and 4th battalions. This was black, red and white and featured a scroll with text specific to each battalion.

With all their training completed and their special equipment with them, the Rangers looked to their front and the dawn of D-Day. Though they had been briefed, what they did not know was just how well the defenders of Pointe du Hoc would react.

The German Army personnel defending the D-Day beaches against the attacking Allied troops were a mix of veterans and well-trained soldiers.

4

THE DEFENDERS

Waiting behind Pointe du Hoc for the US forces heading for Omaha beach were elements of the 352nd Infantry Division of the German Army - prepared for full attack mode, not just static defence. Allied planners had perceived that an over-extended enemy coastal division would provide little opposition from positions overlooking the beaches. Well, there were 'static' defenders from the 716th Coastal Defence Division on Pointe du Hoc, including approximately 120 men of the of the 726th Infantry Regiment and the 2nd Battery of the 1260th Coastal Artillery Regiment manning the 155mm guns. The 716th Division contained many older soldiers from northern Germany but the 352nd Division was of a different calibre of men and they had been inserted to the left of 716th. Covering the area behind the Pointe was the 914th Grenadier Regiment of the 352nd Division. The division contained many men from the 268th and 321st Infantry Divisions that had been withdrawn from Army Group Centre in Russia. The tough Eastern Front-experienced troops provided the basis for the 352nd Division when it was formed

LEFT: When first built the battery at Pointe du Hoc was made up of six open concrete gun pits, with 155mm howitzers mounted on manually operated turntables. *(LHF)*

ABOVE and ABOVE RIGHT: German troops of the Coastal Defence Division on exercise prior to the landings. *(AN)*

in November 1943 and initially employed around the St.Lô area of Normandy. Though some Allied staff suspected that the 352nd had been moved forward, at the time they were far more worried about 21st Panzer Division tank tracks that could suggest a forward move to near the beaches. Fortunately, they were withdrawn to their Caen region locations. Among the 'static' units were some 'volunteer' formations, many of them from Eastern states over-run by the Germans. Some fought well at Normandy; others could not wait to surrender. They had a mixed bag of weapons, some

captured, but the 352nd Infantry Division had a full complement of nine rifle battalions in three regiments according to *D-Day Normandy* (1994). The men were a mix of veterans and well-trained recruits.

The bolt-action 7.92 mm Mauser Kar 98 had been in service with the Germans since World War One, and with modifications, was still the infantry rifle for the *Wehrmacht* until 1945.

The machine pistol MP38 with a 9mm Parabellum round and a 32 round magazine was called, incorrectly, 'Schmeisser' by Allied troops and this automatic weapon was

RIGHT: The command bunker at Pointe du Hoc which allowed views over both Utah and Omaha beaches. At right is the post which disappeared, along with a large piece of the Pointe, into the sea, after bombing by Allied aircraft. *(LHF)*

LEFT: A 155mm howitzer in a gun pit. At left is the entrance to the gun crew's shelter. The gun could be towed out up a slope at the rear of the emplacement. *(LHF)*

particularly useful in fighting in urban environs. In machine guns, the Germans were well served initially by the model designed and manufactured in Switzerland by Solothurn, which was purchased by the German company Rheinmetall-Borsig, when treaty restrictions meant that the German company could not produce embargoed weapons. When they did, the original Model 30 was redesigned as the MG34, using a 7.92mm Mauser round in 50-round belt or a 75-round drum. The rate of fire was 900 rounds per minute (rpm) and excellent though the weapon was, it was expensive to produce - in terms of money and time. So the Germans, through the Mauser company set

about a redesign which produced the MG42 - with the same cartridge, 50-round belts and a rate of fire increase to 1200 rpm. It was easier to mass produce and when the new German Army was formed in the 1950s, the weapon was put back into production because they did not believe there was a better gun.
In Normandy, the German infantry had two types of grenade: the *Eihandgranate 39*, egg shaped, and the *Stielhandgranate 39* - better known as a stick grenade, or to Allied troops t he 'potato masher' because of its shape. After D-Day, British and American armoured units were to feel the effect of a magnetic hand grenade for anti-tank useage. This was the *Heft*

LEFT: One of the gun pits for a 155mm howitzer at Pointe du Hoc. The gun is shrouded in camouflage net. Construction of the battery appears to be at an early stage. *(LHF)*

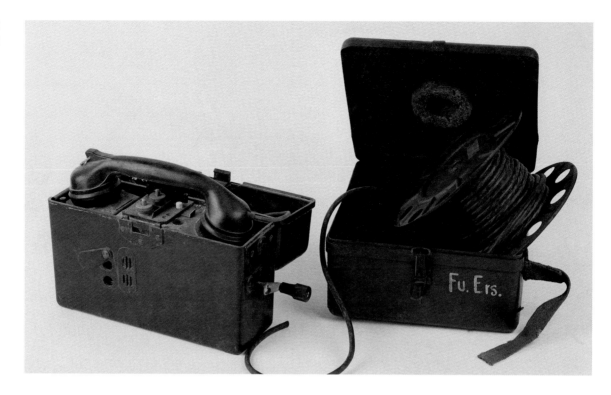

Hohlladunggranate 3kg. It took a very brave soldier to use it! Other anti-tank weapons included the *PanzerabwehrKanone* (PaK) 38, the more powerful PaK 40, and the one that most Allied tank troops feared - the 88mm PaK 43. Introduced into Normandy was the *Panzerfaust*, a disposable, shoulder-launched anti-tank weapon. The artillery pieces, those waiting on or near the coast for targets, or those batteries further inland, are too numerous to mention.

The Rangers had some extra-special equipment, and so did the defenders with a variety of mines and obstacles designed to make life difficult for any incoming troops.

Historian Ambrose summed up the difficulties facing any first-wave soldier whose destination was Omaha beach. "He would have to get through the minefields in the Channel without his LST blowing up, then get from ship to shore in a Higgins boat taking fire from inland batteries, then work his way through an obstacle-studded tidal flat of some 164yds (150m) criss-crossed by machine-gun and rifle fire, with big shells whistling by and mortars exploding all around, to find his first protection behind the shingle. There he would be caught in a triple crossfire – machine guns and heavy artillery from the sides, small arms from the front, mortars coming down from above.

LEFT: The 7.92mm MG42 was an excellent light machine gun. The weapon had a rate of fire of up to 1,200 rounds per minute from 50-round ammunition belts. (JSS)

BELOW: The 7.92mm Mauser Kar 98K was the standard German infantry rifle. The upper illustration shows the weapon fitted with a launcher and an anti-tank grenade. The lower illustration is of the standard Kar 98K with a munitions round and a S.84/98 bayonet. (JSS)

"If the GI was not killed getting off his landing craft or crossing the tidal flat, if by some miracle he made it to the shingle, Rommel (Field Marshal Erwin, in command of Normandy defences) wanted him wounded before he got there. If not wounded, paralyzed by fear. To keep that GI huddled there, Rommel had more mines laid. Between the shingle and the bluffs there was a shelf of beach flat (in some places marshy). Rommel loaded in the barbed wire but relied mainly on mines. They were irregularly placed throughout the shelf and were of all types. Some were simple charges of TNT covered by rock and set off by trip wires. S-mines were devices of the devil; they jumped up when activated, then exploded at waist height. There were others.

RIGHT: The 9mm
MP 40 sub-machine
gun. Fabricated
from metal and
plastic, it was
probably the best
weapon of its type
in World War Two
and was produced
from 1940 to 1945.
(JSS)

RIGHT: The 9mm
MP 40 sub-machine
gun. Fabricated
from metal and
plastic, it was
probably the best
weapon of its type
in World War Two
and was produced
from 1940 to 1945.
(JSS)

BELOW: The fast
firing 7.92mm
*Maschinengewehr
42* (MG 42) light
machine gun
mounted on the
standard tripod.
At Pointe du Hoc
there were two
fixed machine
gun posts which
would have been
equipped with this
weapon. (JSS)

Altogether Rommel's forces laid 6.5 million mines, and wanted many millions more (his goal was 11 million anti-personnel mines). Behind the mines and astride the draws there were anti-tank ditches, two meters (6.7ft) or so deep, and cement anti-tank or anti-truck barriers across the exit roads".

As Ambrose stressed, once behind Omaha, once inland the soldiers would not face fixed defenses of any kind "but as every GI who fought in Normandy can testify, in the country of hedgerows and stone-walled villages, farmhouses, barns, and outbuildings, fixed fortifications were not needed. The hedgerow country of Normandy was ideal for fighting a defensive struggle with the weapons of the mid-twentieth century".

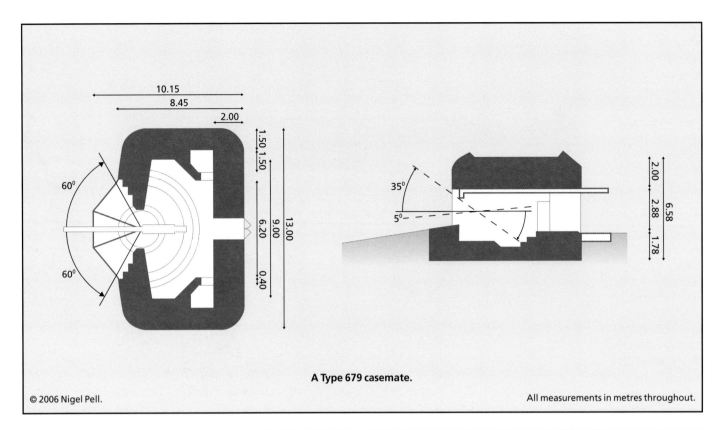

A Type 679 casemate.

All measurements in metres throughout.

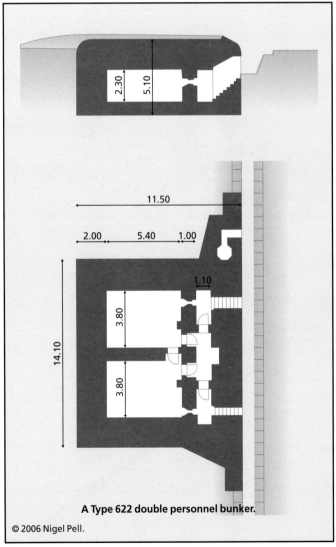

A Type 622 double personnel bunker.

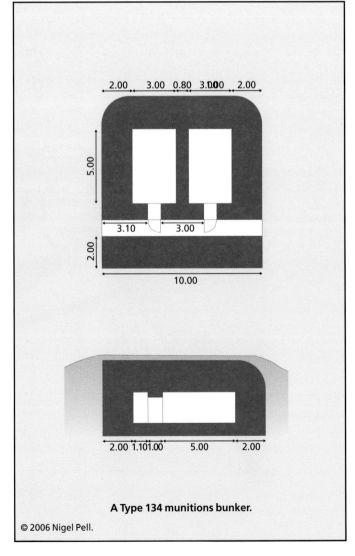

A Type 134 munitions bunker.

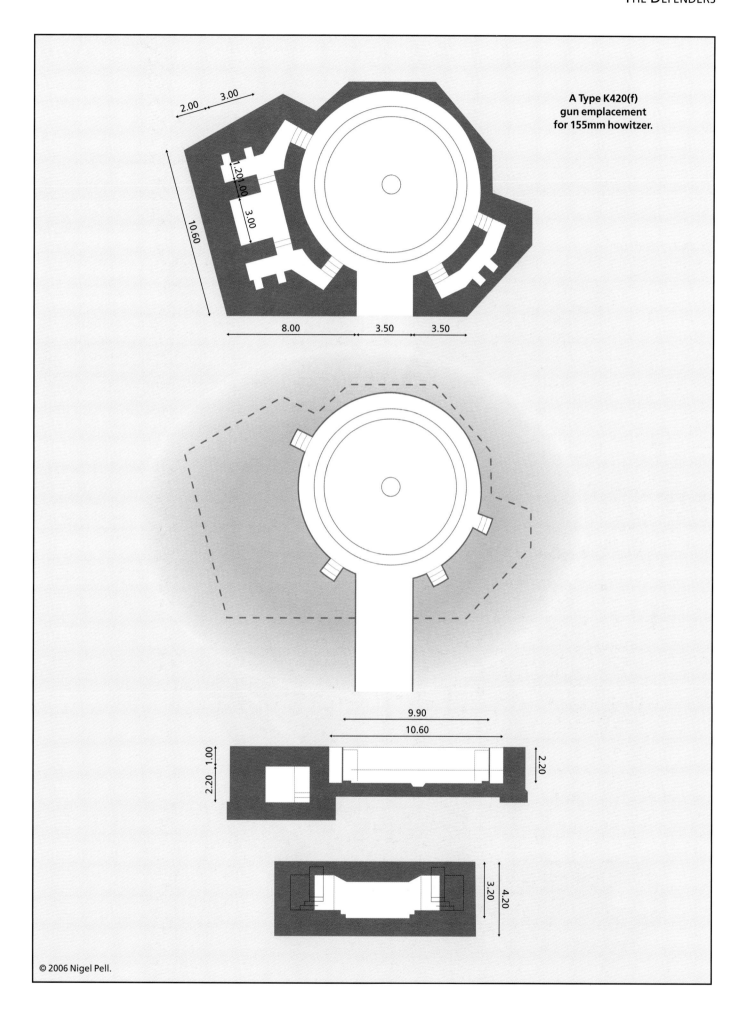

A Type K420(f)
gun emplacement
for 155mm howitzer.

LEFT: The 9mm Luger Model 1908 was in German service from World War One until 1938 but many were used during World War Two. The pistol was originally made by Deutsche Waffen und Munitions-fabrik (DWM) and then by Mauser. A later model, the 7.65mm, was almost identical. Below is the 9mm Walther P38 which was to replace the Luger as the standard German service pistol. The magazine held eight rounds and the weapon's double-action design allowed it to be safely carried with a round in the firing chamber. (JSS)

LEFT: A standard German Army 50mm W36 light mortar. (JSS)

RIGHT: The 81mm W34 mortar. This weapon was the standard medium infantry mortar for the German Army. *(JSS)*

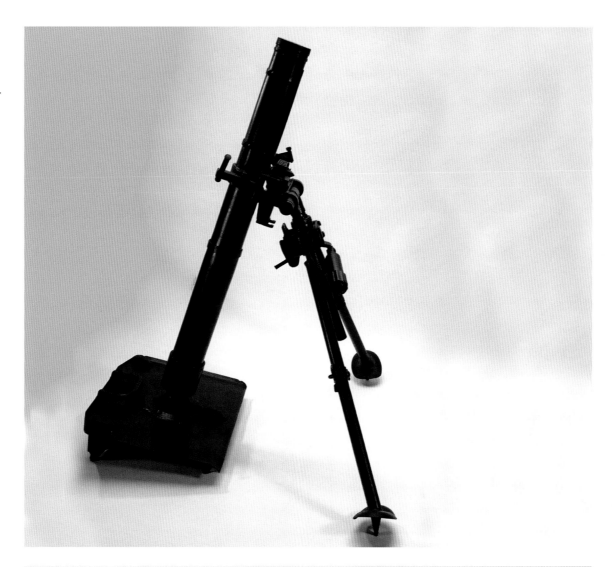

RIGHT: German stick grenades in the pressed steel carrying case. German grenades relied on explosive power rather than the fragmentation of the types used by the Allied armies. *(JSS)*

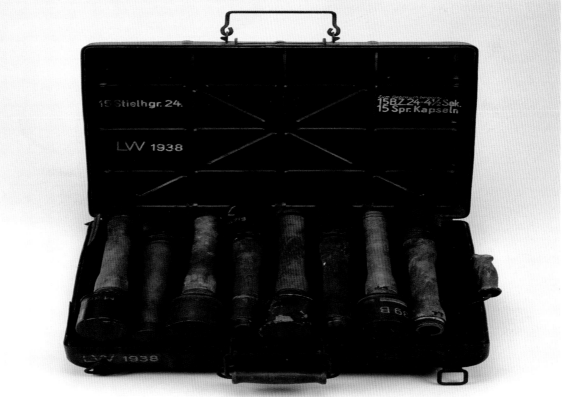

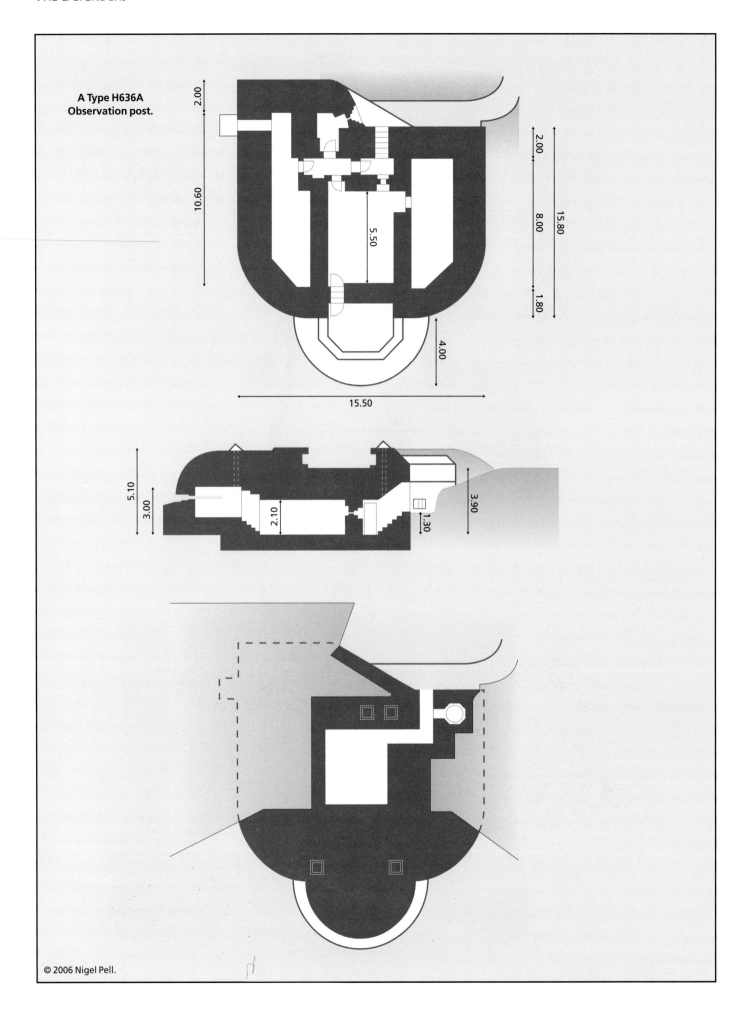

**A Type H636A
Observation post.**

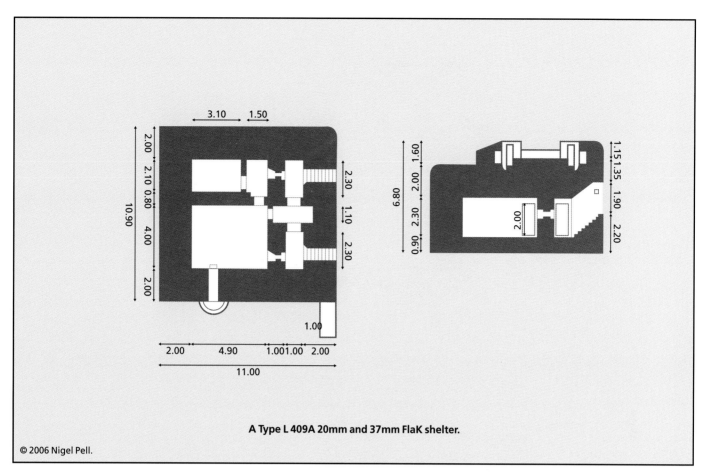

A Type L 409A 20mm and 37mm FlaK shelter.

© 2006 Nigel Pell.

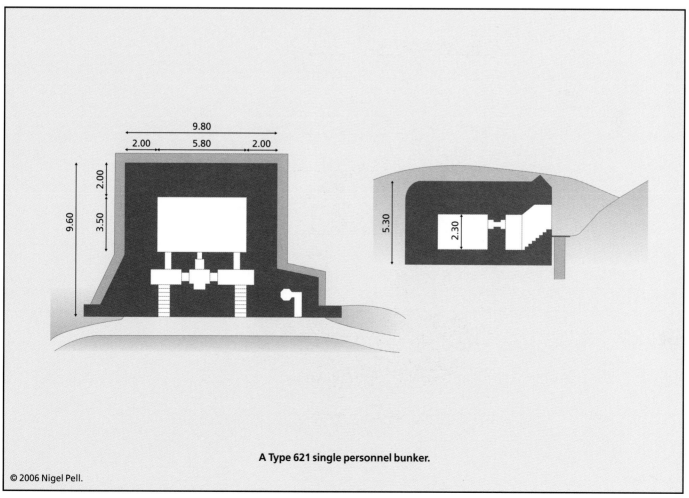

A Type 621 single personnel bunker.

© 2006 Nigel Pell.

Douglas A-20B Havoc medium bombers over Pointe du Hoc. **A** indicates the position of the 155mm Howitzer battery. *(AN)*

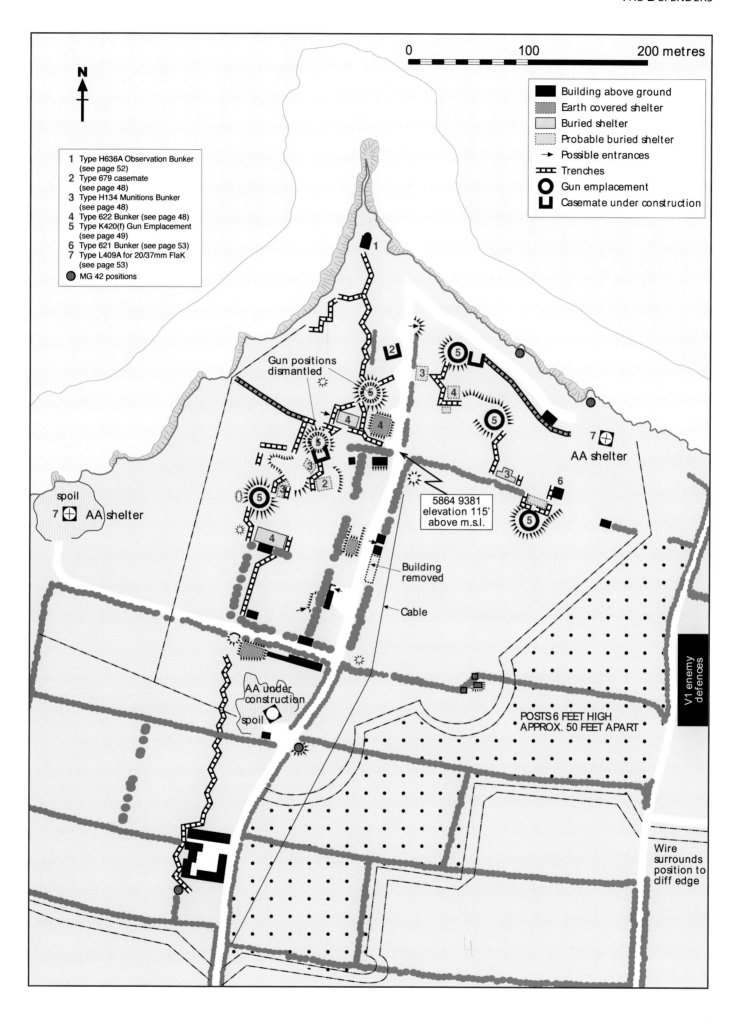

0   100   200 metres

■ Building above ground
▨ Earth covered shelter
▨ Buried shelter
▨ Probable buried shelter
→ Possible entrances
⊞ Trenches
⊂⊃ Gun emplacement
⊏⊐ Casemate under construction

1 Type H636A Observation Bunker
   (see page 52)
2 Type 679 casemate
   (see page 48)
3 Type H134 Munitions Bunker
   (see page 48)
4 Type 622 Bunker (see page 48)
5 Type K420(f) Gun Emplacement
   (see page 49)
6 Type 621 Bunker (see page 53)
7 Type L409A for 20/37mm FlaK
   (see page 53)
● MG 42 positions

N

Gun positions
dismantled

spoil
7 ⊕ AA shelter

7 ⊕
AA shelter

5864 9381
elevation 115'
above m.s.l.

Building
removed

Cable

AA under
construction
spoil

POSTS 6 FEET HIGH
APPROX. 50 FEET APART

V1 enemy
defences

Wire
surrounds
position to
cliff edge

55

Aerial reconnaissance photograph at low tide of Pointe du Hoc battery, a few days before the Rangers landing on 6 June 1944, after many attacks by Allied bombers. The apparent devastation was added to by pre-invasion naval gunfire but the concrete emplacements were solid enough to protect many of the defenders. *(CCM)*

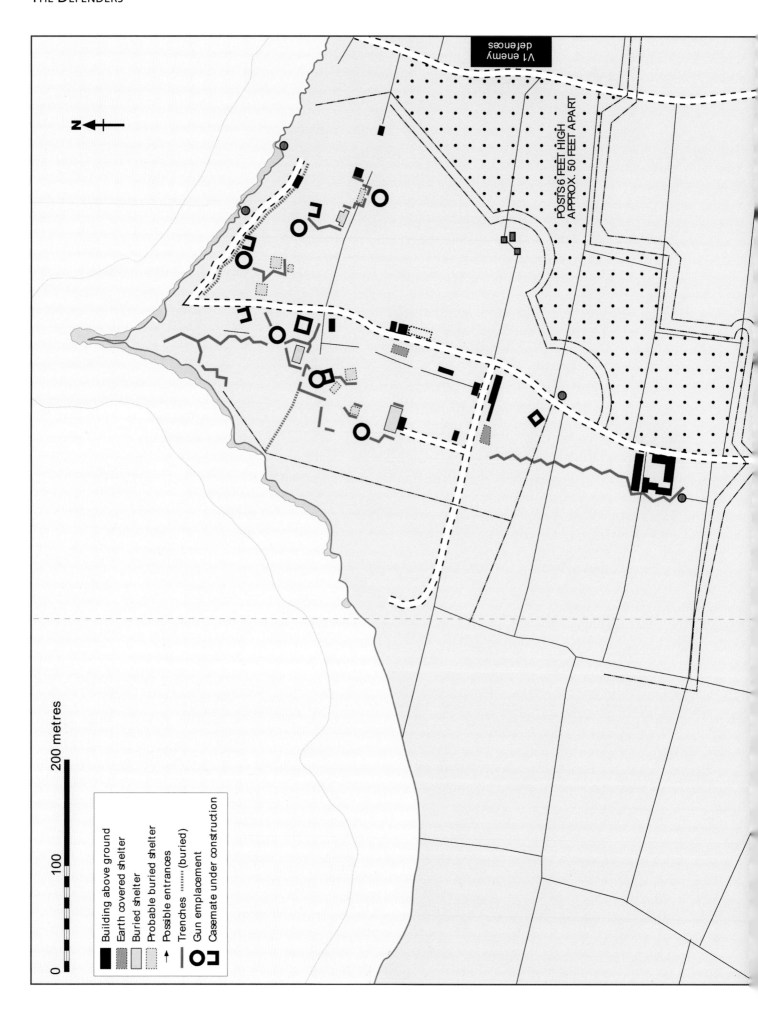

V1 enemy
defences

POSTS 6 FEET HIGH
APPROX. 50 FEET APART

N

200 metres

0   100

Building above ground
Earth covered shelter
Buried shelter
Probable buried shelter
Possible entrances
Trenches ······· (buried)
Gun emplacement
Casemate under construction

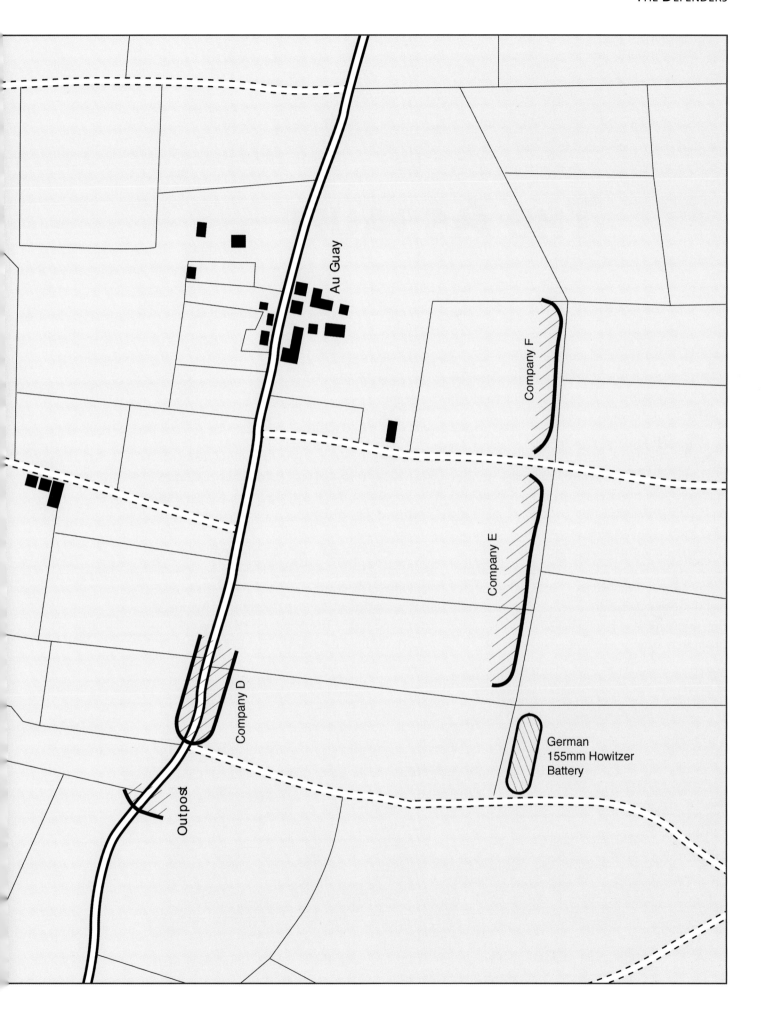

Au Guay

Company F

Company E

Company D

Outpost

German
155mm Howitzer
Battery

For Lt.-Col. James Rudder one decision he made before departure from England was to lead his Rangers in the attack – and defy his divisional commander.

THE ASSAULT

German Field Marshal Count Helmuth Karl Bernard von Moltke (1800-1891) is credited with the classic military warning - 'no plan survives contact with the enemy'. More precisely in *Kriegsgeschichtiche Einzelschriften* (1880) he wrote: "No plan of operations reaches with any certainty beyond the first encounter with the enemy's main force". As far as 2nd Ranger Battalion members were concerned, plans for D-Day were encountering difficulties before they even left the safety of the English coast. A recently promoted officer was supposed to lead the assault by companies D, E and F - but he "unfortunately managed to get himself thoroughly drunk and unruly while still aboard his transport in Weymouth harbour" Lt James W. Eikner wrote in a 1993 letter to Stephen Ambrose. The offending officer was returned to shore and the Rangers never saw him again. This brought about a major change to the plan. Lt.-Col. Rudder decided he would lead the cliff climbing men; not a decision that appealed to Lt-Gen. Clarence Huebner, commanding the US Army's 1st Division and in overall command of the Omaha Beach. He told

LEFT: Loading supplies on to LCAs at Weymouth Harbour, Dorset, in the southwest of England. *(WyM)*

RIGHT: Rangers embarking on to Landing Craft Assault (LCA) at Weymouth. All LCAs were crewed by Royal Navy personnel. *(WyM)*

Rudder that he didn't want the colonel knocked out in the first round. Rudder replied "I'm sorry to disobey you, sir, but if I don't take it, it may not go".

Companies D, E and F were delighted that their boss was with them. The next problem was one of location identification as the LCAs, to Rudder's dismay, were going straight for Pointe de la Percée and the time was 06.30 - when they should have been hitting a beach nearly four miles (6.44km) to the west. In 1945 the Historical Division of the US War Department in Washington published a

detailed account of D-Day in a series entitled *American Forces in Action*. There have been facsimile reprints in three years since then and the accounts can now be read on the Internet. The description of the Rangers' trials and tribulations before reaching their target is a classic of understatement: "Their assault plan provided for landing at H Hour, Companies E and F on the east side of the Point, Company D to the west.

Unfortunately, one of the accidents of misdirection befell the Rangers; they headed eastward so far that, when the mistake was

RIGHT: Loading supplies on to LCAs at Weymouth Harbour. On the stern can be seen the lettering PM denoting that they are from HMS *Princess Maud* which carried the Ranger's Special Engineers Task Force (SETF) to Omaha beach. *(WyM)*

ABOVE: LCAs were built in England to the basic hull design of Andrew Higgins. The British added light armour plating to the bows and gunwhales. These additions made the vessel heavier thus reducing speed and manoeuvreability. The letters PC denote that this LCA is from HMS *Prince Charles*. *(WyM)*

corrected, they had to approach the Pointe from that quarter on a course close to and almost paralleling the shore. Under fire from strong points along the cliffs, the flotilla came in 40 minutes late. This delay meant that the eight other companies of Rangers (A and B of the 2nd Battalion, and the entire 5th Battalion),waiting off shore for word of the assault, did not follow in to Pointe du Hoe [sic] but went toward Vierville". Lt. Eikner, already mentioned and Rudder's communications officer, giving oral history evidence to the Eisenhower Center recalled "bailing water with our helmets, dodging bullets, and vomiting all at the same time". One of the four DUKWs was sunk by a 20mm shell. The Rangers must have felt like human targets, powerless to do anything about the incoming fire as their craft made slow headway against the tide. They had already lost one LCA, swamped by water though the officer commanding, Capt 'Duke' Slater and his men were picked up by an LCT. They wanted to get into the action but a medical officer, seeing they were badly affected by the freezing cold water, ordered their return to England. Meanwhile, Rudder had waved the two other Company D LCAs to join in the

assault from the east - not from the west of the Pointe, as planned.

The progress of the LCAs carrying Task Force A was as follows: -

Supply LCA 914 and LCA 860- abandoned and sank before landing.

Company D's LCA 668 and 858 originally to land on the westside of the Pointe were forced to land on the east side.

Company E and HQ's LCA 722 containing medical personnel sent message to Task Force B at 07.30.

LCA 888 Rudder's craft was first to land at 07.10.

LCA 861 was the second LCA to land.

LCA 862 contained the naval shore fire control party.

Company F's LCA 884 and LCA 887 landed without incident.

LCA 883 was the last to beach.

LCT 415 launched four DUKWs, two mounted with the ex-fire brigade ladders and two in support 4,000 yd (3,658m) from the beach.

On the unplanned run-in towards Pointe du Hoc, Sgt. Bill Petty occasionally risked popping his head above the side of his LCA, but mainly -

ABOVE: Men of the 2nd Ranger Battalion embarking on LCAs at Weymouth, Dorset. *(WyM)*

LEFT: Lt. James Eikner was Col. Rudder's communications officer. Note the Ranger badge on the shoulder of his tunic. *(WyM)*

ABOVE and RIGHT:
Conditions on
board an LCA
were very cramped
for the Rangers,
making emergency
exit very difficult.
(WyM)

ABOVE and LEFT: Rangers on board an LCA. Note two have the Ranger badge, a blue diamond with yellow edging and lettering on the left shoulder. One is armed with a US Army standard portable flame-thrower M1A1 which required two men to operate. *(USN)*

and wisely - kept his head down as bullets hammered against the armoured protection. Fortunately, two destroyers could see the predicament of the Ranger Task Force A. The USS *Satterlee* (DD 626) and HMS *Talybont* watched the German defenders on the cliff tops emerging when the heavy bombardment from the 10 x 14in guns of USS *Texas*, the oldest warship in the US Navy fleet (commissioned in 1914), had ceased. Both *Satterlee* and *Talybont* had supported USS *Texas* in the opening bombardment.

The USS *Satterlee*, a Gleaves-class destroyer was built by Seattle-Tacoma Shipbuilding Corporation of Seattle, Washington state and carried four 5-inch guns and smaller weaponry. The Gleaves-class destroyer was commissioned on 1 July 1943 and sold for scrap on 8 May 1972. The Royal Navy Hunt-class (Type III) HMS *Talybont* was built by J. Samuel White & Company of Cowes on the Isle of Wight and commissioned on 19 May 1943.

On D-Day, the commanding officers and crews of *Satterlee* and *Talybont* did their best to

support the Rangers - and with a persistent fire on the defenders, kept their heads down for most of the time ...time that was so precious to the US elite soldiers. Fifty years after serving Lt. George Kerchner, Company D, 2nd Ranger Battalion, went on record for the Eisenhower Center and said: "Some day I would love to meet up with somebody from Satterlee so I can shake his hand and thank him". The US Navy destroyers were supposed to save some of their ammunition while on station in case the German Navy tried a surprise attack but most returned to England with no ammunition, or precious little left. *Satterlee* had fired over 600 rounds and went back empty.

The nine surviving LCAs hit the beach on a 400-yard (366m) front on the east side of the Pointe. The naval gunfire had lifted at H Hour, for obvious reasons but as has been mentioned, Task Force A was 40 minutes late in arriving - time the defenders had used to recover and to man the trenches above the cliff.

Despite heavy gunfire from USS *Satterlee*, as the *American Forces In Action* records: -

LEFT: HMS *Talybont*, a Hunt-class (Type III) destroyer. The vessel was built by J. Samuel White at Cowes, Isle of Wight, and commissioned into service on 19 May 1943. She was armed with four 4-inch guns in two turrets, one 'PomPom' in a quadruple mount and three 20mm Oerlikon cannons. *(RNM)*

ABOVE: USS *Satterlee* (DD 626), a Gleaves-class destroyer. The vessel was armed with four 5-inch guns in four turrets and six .50 calibre heavy machine guns. On 30 May 1945 she was, after modification, recommissioned as DMS 38, a fast minesweeper. The vessel was scrapped 8 May 1972. *(USN)*

"scattered small-arms fire and automatic fire from a flanking machine-gun position beat around the LCAs, causing about 15 casualties as the Rangers debarked on the heavily cratered strip of beach. The rockets had been fired immediately on touchdown. Some of the water-soaked ropes failed to carry over the cliff, but only one craft failed to get at least one grapnel to the edge. In one or two cases, the demountable extension ladders were used. The DUKWs came in but could not get across the cratered beach, and from the water's edge their extension ladders would not reach the top of the cliff". With the benefit of hindsight, we now know that only one fire service extension ladder could be used and in action, that must have seemed like a scene from an early black and white silent comedy movie. Had it not been so serious. And there was anything but silence as the Germans tried to stop the Rangers with rifle, machine gun fire, grenades and even artillery shells dangling on the cliff face and awaiting detonation at the right moment. One 200mm shell did explode, and Rudder was knocked off the cliff by a resulting rock fall and other Rangers, if they had time, wondered how

on earth Sgt. William Stivison survived at the top of the extension ladder that was erected - albeit in a very rickety fashion. Stephen Ambrose recaptured the scene well in D-Day: "He (Stivison) was swaying back and forth like a metronome, German tracers whipping about him" and he quoted Lt. Elmer Vermeer: "The ladder was swaying at about a forty-five degree angle - both ways. Stivison would fire short bursts as he passed over the cliff at the top of the arch, but the DUKW floundered so badly that they had to bring the fire ladder back down".

Naval gunfire and USAF and RAF bombing not only cratered the surface of Pointe du Hoc, and removed some of the cliff face but the damage also affected the beach area with the large indentations making life difficult for LCAs and the DUKWs. It was not all bad, because the 'softening up' process had also produced some mounds at the base of the cliffs, and one gave the Rangers a 40ft. (36.6m) start in their climb. As mentioned, the ropes with grappling hooks to be fired by rockets from LCAs had suffered so much from water the extra weight prevented some reaching the top. The hand-held launchers worked much better.

The scene re-created in *The Longest Day* film, showing the defenders doing their utmost to cut the ropes, gives a really graphic illustration of the problems for both sides.

Fifteen men of Task Force A became casualties - two of them Lt. Kerchner's men, hit by enfilading (defenders firing along the lines of defence) machine gun fire. Feeling angry, the young officer picked up a dead Ranger's rifle in an effort to avenge his men - then realised his first task was to get to the top of the cliff. Other men started to climb the cliff, some using ropes, some digging in knives or bayonets to haul themselves up. As Kerchner said, it was not necessary to tell the men what to do - "they had been trained, they had the order in which they were supposed to climb the ropes and the men were all moving right in and starting to climb up the cliff". Kerchner, in command of Company D as a result of the commander's LCA sinking, found the climb very easy, "much easier than some of the climbs in England". The Rangers reached the top faster than expected. It is thought the first man to do so managed the climb in five minutes and the

ABOVE: USS *Satterlee* (DD 626) in Belfast Lough, Northern Ireland, 14 May 1944. In the background are USS *Baldwin* (DD 624) and USS *Nelson* (DD 623). All are part of Destroyer Division 36, Destroyer Squadron 18 of the US Navy's Atlantic Fleet. *(USN)*

LEFT: In preparation for D-Day USS *Nevada* (BB 36) was deployed with other units of the US Navy to Belfast Lough, Northern Ireland, 14 May 1944. In the background is USS *Texas* (BB 35). Both ships bombarded German shore-based targets along Omaha Beach prior to the landings on 6 June 1944. *(USN)*

ABOVE: USS *Nevada* (BB 36) fires a broadside over the heads of US forces on Omaha Beach, 6 June 1944. *(USN)*

LEFT: Landing Craft Infantry (LCI) under way to Omaha Beach, 6 June 1944. The photograph was taken from the deck of USS *Ancon* (AGC-4). *(USN)*

ABOVE: *Ancon* was a passenger liner until 1942, when it became US Army Transport USS *Ancon* (AP-66). On 8 May 1943 USS *Ancon* entered service, after conversion, as an amphibious command ship (AGC-4). This photograph dated 11 June 1943 shows the ship during preparations for the Allied landings on Sicily. *(USN)*

LEFT: USS *Ancon* (AGC-4) was the command ship for the Omaha Beach landing. In the foreground is patrol craft USS *PC 564*. The photograph is dated 7 June 1944. *(USN)*

ABOVE: The result of naval gunfire on Vierville to the west of Pointe du Hoc. The church spire, which was an MG and observation post, was attacked with the guns of USS *Harding* (DD 625) and destroyed. *(USN)*

LEFT: A Gleave-class destroyer (possibly USS *Satterlee*) shelling German positions with its four 5-inch guns. Two other US Navy destroyers, USS *Thompson* and USS *Harding,* were involved in action on the sector from Vierville to Pointe du Hoc. The Royal Navy destroyer HMS *Talybont* was also involved. *(USN)*

surviving members of the force were all up in 30 minutes. Some had to make several attempts, especially when the Germans succeeded in cutting ropes. Stephen Ambrose tells of Sgt. Petty's anger when, having had problems with a wet and very slippery rope, he was told by medical officer Capt. Walter Block to get up to the top of the cliff. "I've been trying to get up this goddamned rope for five minutes and if you think you can do any better you can f***ing well do it yourself". Block is reported to have turned away, trying to control his own temper! He also had some crucial work to do as the casualties mounted.

Ranger Alban Meccia is quoted in Russell Miller's *Nothing Less Than Victory* (1993): "When we climbed, the Germans shot down at us. Finally, we threw grenades at the cliff, making furrows up the side and giving us some protection. Then we all went up and chased those Germans, killing a lot of them. They had left a

little dog up there in a shack. He would respond to English, but he would stand up when you talked to him in German ...but that dog turned out to be a fifth columnist. He licked the wounded and annoyed them until we had to slit his throat. I saw a German officer shoot one of his men in the back when he started to walk over to us with his hands up. One of our guys saw a flag of surrender, and stood up to wave to the Germans to come over, and was shot between the eyes".

Once on the top of Pointe du Hoc, the Rangers found another advantage from the results of bombing and bombardment - the lunar landscape of craters within a few steps of each other gave excellent cover for fire and manoeuvre as they dealt with the defenders. Sgt. Leonard Lomell also features in *Nothing Less Than Victory*: "Captain Baugh of Company E was the first person I ran across on top. He had been shot and had his hand practically blown off and wasn't in such good shape. We kept right on going

saying, "Captain, we'll send you back a medic". My platoon couldn't wait for nothing. We had our assignment and we in Company D depended on a lot of speed. My second platoon went ahead in a rush. We had some confrontations coming out of shell craters. As we were charging out of a shell crater, a machine gun opened up and Morris Webb, one of my sergeants, jumped back into the crater right on top of one of his men's bayonet that went right through his side.

"We didn't stop; we played it just like a football game, charging hard and low. We went into the shell craters for protection because there were snipers around and machine guns firing at us. We'd wait for a moment and if the fire lifted we were out of that crater and into the next one. We ran as fast as we could over to the gun positions - to the one that we were assigned to. There were no guns in the positions! "There was an anti-aircraft position off to our right several hundred yards and a machine gun

off to the left. There was another machine gun that we had gotten on our way in. The anti-aircraft gun was firing flat trajectory at us and by the time we got to the road I only had about a dozen men left".

Not seeing the expected 155 mm guns must have been a tremendous shock. As *American Forces In Action* says, the Rangers "found themselves in a no-man's land of incredible destruction, all landmarks gone, and the ground so cratered that if men got 15 feet (4.57m) apart they were immediately out of contact. Only a few enemy were seen, and these were quickly driven to cover in a network of ruined trenches connecting deep dugouts and emplacements. One after another, the small advance parties reached their appointed gun emplacements, only to find them empty. The gun positions, three of them casemated, were partly wrecked; the guns had been removed. Without hesitation, the Ranger parties started inland on their next mission: to reach the coastal highway, set up a defensive position cutting that main route between Vierville and Grandcamp, and await the arrival of the 116th Infantry from Omaha Beach".

Cornelius Ryan wrote the impressive *The Longest Day* that formed the basis of the film of the same name. He also managed to upset Rangers veterans by pointing out that they "would lose 135 men out of 225 in their heroic attack to silence guns that had never been there". Ryan claimed a French resistance worker, Jean Marion, had tried to point out the absence of the guns to the allies but by the time the message reached Gen. Bradley's staff, the troops were in their sealed locations awaiting departure for Normandy. Later in his book, mentioning the surprise awaiting Task Force A men on the top of Pointe du Hoc, Ryan claimed the guns had never been mounted, adding in a footnote: "Some two hours later (after arriving on the top) a Ranger patrol found a deserted five-gun battery in a camouflaged position more than a mile inland. Stacks of shells surrounded each gun and they were ready to fire, but the Rangers could find no evidence that they had ever been manned. Presumably these were the guns for the Pointe du Hoc emplacements". Fellow historian Stephen Ambrose claims that telegraph poles represented guns in the casemates - but tracks leading inland suggested the guns had been moved. Each platoon had been given a gun position to 'take out' and they set about this without any further orders being required. Some accounts say the guns were moved on 3 June.

The July 2001 edition of *World War II Magazine* carried an article by Michael H. Frederick and Joseph F. Masci, claiming that 55 years after the event 2nd Ranger Battalion is still fighting - "this time to get the truth out about what took place at Pointe-du-Hoc in Normandy". Ryan had implied that the Ranger mission to destroy the German gun battery at Pointe-du-Hoc was a wasted effort. In fact, 1st Sgt. Leonard Lomell of Toms River, N.J.(New Jersey) and Staff Sgt. Jack Kuhn of Altoona, Pa (Pennsylvania), "personally saw to it that the Ranger mission was accomplished early on the morning of June 6, 1944", the authors wrote.

Lomell said: "The section sergeants took charge of the roadblock, and Jack and I decided to take a look at the sunken secondary road.

So we just took the road inland. We thought there might be evidence of tracking and vehicle use. The guns had to have been taken off the Pointe".

After a while, the pair used a hedgerow for cover, and Lomell added: "When it became my turn to look over, I said, 'God, here they are!' They were in an orchard, camouflaged in among the trees. Now, when you camouflage

ABOVE: A Landing Craft Vehicle Personnel (LCVP) 'Higgins Boat'. The vessel was designed by Andrew Higgins and his company built 20,000 at a factory in New Orleans. *(USN)*

five big howitzers, 5-inch guns, these are not ordinary, run-of-the-mill artillery that you cart around behind jeeps. These had stabilizers and everything on them. People say we took them out with fragmentation grenades. That's not so. We couldn't even reach the muzzles. Where they protruded out of the orchard they had netting over them. That's why the aerial photographs never indicated that they were there".

Not with their guns, but not far away were some Germans but the Americans said the gun positions were 'textbook' and had probably not fired because their observation post on Pointe du Hoc had been captured by 2nd Ranger Battalion. The Germans watched by Lomell and Kuhn seemed very nonchalant. The two Rangers approached the guns with thermite grenades - a silent weapon which

ABOVE:
Reinforcements
arrive along the
narrow beach at
Pointe du Hoc.
(USN)

LEFT: The cliff face
at Pointe du Hoc.
Note the toggled
rope and the
lightweight
tubular-steel
ladder. The Ranger
to the right is
carrying a
Browning
Automatic Rifle
(BAR). *(USN)*

generates an amazing amount of heat sufficient to weld important moving parts together. After putting two guns out of action, and smashing five gunsights with his Tommy gun wrapped in his field jacket, Lomell decided more grenades were essential. Other US troops manning the road-block handed over their supply of thermite grenades and, as Lomell recalled: "That moving, flowing molten metal, wherever it eventually got to, must have done the trick. I don't think I spent 10 minutes, all told, destroying those guns. I was satisfied that I had done what I was trained to do. We never looked back. We didn't waste a second".

Running back to their fellow Rangers, Kuhn and Lomell were hurled into the air by a huge explosion but survived without injury. Asked what other Rangers thought when they returned, Kuhn said: "First of all, they didn't know what we had done. They heard this explosion and …I remember Pte Larry Johnson, I could have hugged him. He was all

by himself there at the road intersection. He said: 'What the hell was that?' I said: 'We don't know but, Larry, the guns are inoperative'. Unfortunately, Larry was killed on another day. I can't understand why a German patrol wasn't dispatched after that to see what the heck the explosion was and what was up there at the intersection".

The explosion was the result of a huge pile of ammunition being destroyed by high-explosive charges laid by a patrol led by Sgt. Frank Lupinski.

Well as Kuhn and Lomell had done, the position on Pointe du Hoc was not secure and there were still some pockets of resistance in what Lt. Kerchner discovered was a self-contained fort, including an 8ft (2.44m) deep zig-zag trench, the deepest he had ever seen. Using their variety of weapons the Rangers pushed the garrison back but the closer they got to the perimeter the tougher the opposition got. They killed or captured Germans - and

Reinforcements arrive at Pointe du Hoc. The mound of rubble in the fore-ground is the part of the Pointe which collapsed. It helped in the Ranger's ascent of the cliff. *(USN)*

ABOVE: Rangers relax after the attack. The officer at right has a .30in M1/M2 automatic carbine. *(USN)*

suffered casualties themselves. Lt.-Col. Rudder had ordered a signal sent to the reserve of Companies A and B of the 2nd Battalion and the 5th Ranger Battalion to land at Omaha, instead of following their leader to Pointe du Hoc, and to rejoin Companies D, E and F from Vierville, approaching landward from the east. Rudder had moved his command post to the top at 07.45 - 15 minutes after the radio message "Praise the Lord" had gone to inform commanders that Task Force A was literally on top of things. This was true in one sense, not so in another. Twelve late-comers were diverted from going inland and sent to attack the troublesome anti-aircraft position. As *American Forces In Action* records: "As they worked toward it through craters, artillery and mortar fire stopped them and the party

scattered. A few minutes later a German counterattack, emerging from tunnels or nearby trenches, overwhelmed and captured all but one man. So torn up was the ground that the command post group, in a crater only a hundred yards away, was unaware of what had happened until the survivor returned. Another assault was hastily improvised, consisting of a dozen riflemen and a mortar section. They got halfway to the strongpoint and were caught by artillery fire, which killed or wounded nearly every man in the party".

Giving the Rangers a lot of problems was a machine gun on the eastern edge of the site, sweeping the ground as it had swept the beach. Another problem was that the shore-fire control party consisting of an artillery officer and a naval lieutenant could no longer

function because of an 'own goal', an Allied shell that had fallen short. Such sad things happen in war, but sharp thinking individuals can always help and Lt Eikner had brought an old World War One signal lamp with him. He had trained some of the Rangers in Morse code and though they had doubted the wisdom of taking the equipment, it had a tracking device to keep in touch with a ship, a tripod and a telescopic sight.

Eikner and his men did make contact with USS *Satterlee*, made adjustments after fall of shot, and soon the destroyer's 5-inch guns blew the machine gun position off the cliff. Rudder was blown off his feet by the shell from HMS *Glasgow* that killed the shore-fire officer Capt. Harwood and wounded Lt. Norton and soon after that Rudder was shot in the leg by a sniper.

He carried on in control - to the admiration of his officers and men - and was hurt again later in the day by splinters of concrete sent flying by another naval shell. But Rudder redoubled his efforts, inspiring his men in what had now become a siege as Germans reacted to events. Enemy snipers were in action in the fortifications, and despite several attempts, the Rangers still had to completely clear the enemy from the maze of wrecked positions. Three or four Germans still held out on the tip of the Point in an undamaged concrete observation post. The signal lamp was used again to pass a message to *Satterlee* stating 'mission accomplished, many casualties, short of ammunition and need recruits'. An hour later the Rangers were told by Gen Huebner, via the good ship, that no reinforcements were

ABOVE: USS *Harding* (DD 625) was part of Destroyer Division 36, Destroyer Squadron 18, of the US Atlantic Fleet sent to the UK in prepar-ation for the D-Day landings. The ship was converted to a High-Speed Mine-sweeper (DMS 28) in November 1944. In April 1945 the vessel was badly damaged in a Japanese 'Kamikaze' attack. *(USN)*

LEFT: USS *Thompson* (DD 305) in May 1945 after conversion (note the after turret has been replaced with a cable winding drum) to a High-Speed Minesweeper (DMS 38). *(USN)*

ABOVE: HMS *Glasgow*, the seventh ship of that name to serve with the Royal Navy. It was a Southampton-class light cruiser (a sub-class of the Town-class cruiser) and mounted a main armament of eight 4-inch guns in four turrets. *(RNM)*

available. Miraculously, 23 men from Company A, 5th Rangers appeared, led by Lt. Charles H. Parker - and that was by accident, rather than design because Parker and party had become separated from their unit in the shambles of Omaha beach. On arrival at the designated rendezvous (RV) area, as no-one else appeared, Parker and his men wisely headed for Pointe du Hoc, fighting on the way, and even taking prisoners. They learned that Rudder had lost one-third of his men as casualties. Two German counter attacks by the 1st Battalion, 914th Grenadier Regiment of the 352nd Division had been stopped. Other attempts to relieve the Rangers had been beaten back by the Germans and so the battered but determined force now defending their gains; had to spend another night on Pointe du Hoc.

When the second day dawned Rudder had about 90 men able to fight - and some of them wounded - of the original 225 … plus Parker's men and three parachutists who were pleased to find friendly forces, having been lost - as many of those dropped early on D-Day had been. USS *Thompson* had taken over naval gunfire support from *Satterlee* and when *Thompson* had to withdraw USS *Harding* took on the destroyers' vital role of helping the

Rangers fend off the Germans. They, after three more attempts to dislodge the Rangers, withdrew to a new defensive line.

The planned land reinforcements had still not not reached Rudder's men and did not do until the next day, 8 June - almost 48 hours later than scheduled.

What of Companies A, B and C of 2nd Ranger Battalion and the men of 5th Ranger Battalion at Omaha? Task Force B (their role mentioned earlier) suffered - along with all on this notorious beach - from the fierce German defence and had about 65% casualties before reaching the foot of the cliffs. Historian Max Hastings in his book *Overlord* says: "It was a tribute to the quality of the Rangers that despite losses on a scale that stopped many infantry units in their tracks on Omaha that morning, the survivors of C Company pressed on to climb the cliffs west of the beach using bayonets and toggle ropes, clearing German positions one by one in a succession of fierce close-quarter actions with Tommy guns and phosphorous grenades". Insufficient Sherman DD tanks had reached the beaches, thus Company C of the Rangers did not have the numbers, or heavy support needed to get them to Pointe du Hoc. Lt. Sid Salomon looked down

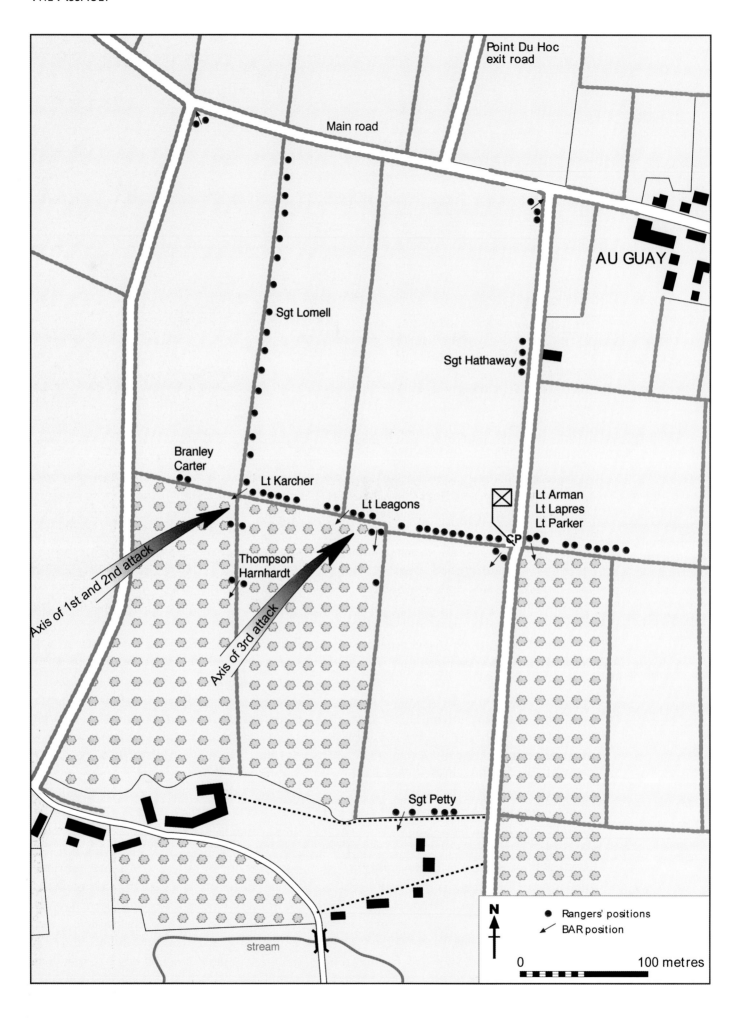

Point Du Hoc
exit road

Main road

Sgt Lomell

AU GUAY

Sgt Hathaway

Branley
Carter

Lt Karcher

Lt Leagons

Lt Arman
Lt Lapres
Lt Parker

CP

Axis of 1st and 2nd attack

Thompson
Harnhardt

Axis of 3rd attack

Sgt Petty

stream

N

● Rangers' positions
↙ BAR position

0   100 metres

RIGHT: One of the 155mm howitzers moved from the battery at Pointe du Hoc and hidden around 1,094yds (1km) inland in an orchard. These were discovered by Sgts Leonard Lomell and Jack Kuhn who destroyed the guns by using thermite grenades. *(AN)*

on the human tragedy and wreckage of war from a captured German position and considered the invasion a failure. He thought it could be a long swim back to England.

Task Force C, two companies of the 2nd Battalion and all of the 5th Battalion, landed more successfully than Company C but were pinned down behind a sea wall and faced with murderous fire. Brigadier General Norman 'Dutch' Cota, deputy commander of the US Army's 29th Division was beginning to think the assault on Omaha would fail and around 10.00 issued his now-famous call 'Rangers, lead the way!' Individual platoons began to move forward off the beach and make for Vierville, the main route to Pointe du Hoc. With what was left of his force and 150 men of the 116th Regimental Combat Team under Lt.-Col. Max Schneider began the march but even with some tanks in support, they

were stopped by very accurate artillery fire near St.Pierre du Mont. They tried again on 8 June and then relieved Rudder and his force.

Of course Task Force A achieved its objectives. As Lt. Eikner said in his oral history interview for the Eisenhower Center: "Had we not been there we felt quite sure that those guns would have been put into operation and they would have brought much death and destruction down on our men on the beaches and our ships at sea. But by 09.00 on D-Day morning, the big guns had been put out of commission and the paved highway had been cut and we had roadblocks denying its use to the enemy. So by 09.00 our mission was accomplished. The Rangers at Pointe du Hoc were the first American forces on D-Day to accomplish their mission and we are proud of that".

After Pointe du Hoc, 2nd Rangers were not used in any further special operations and suffered as a result of the regular soldiers dislike of elite fighting forces.

6

AFTERMATH

Of the 2nd Ranger Battalion involved in the D-Day assault, 77 were killed, 38 reported missing in action and 152 wounded. There were to be no more special operations for the battalion, but service alongside regular infantry units in areas such as the Cherbourg peninsula. Rangers were deployed in 'Operation Cobra' against many objectives in Brittany, France and also in the Huertgen Forest in Germany. Lt.Col. Rudder left six months after D-Day to command the 109th Infantry Regiment. The 2nd Rangers were in Czechoslovakia when the war in Europe ended in May 1945. Thirteen Rangers of the 2nd Battalion were awarded the Distinguished Service Cross (DSC) and a host of awards went to other Rangers. The battalion was awarded a Presidential Unit Citation for the achievements of Pointe du Hoc, as well as a French Croix de Guerre with Silver-Gilt Star. The 2nd Ranger Battalion was deactivated on 23 October 1945 at Camp Patrick Henry, Virginia.

The 5th Ranger Battalion was deactivated on 22 October 1945 at Camp Miles Standish, Massachusetts. The 6th Ranger Battalion

LEFT: After the beachhead was established USN communication posts were set up where radio, signal lamps and even flags (semaphore) were used to contact vessels at sea. *(AN)*

fought on in the Pacific campaign until it, too, was deactivated on 20 December 1945, ending the history of Rangers in World War Two.

Rudder was a full colonel at the end of the war, retired as a major-general US Army Reserve in 1967 and in civilian life became Mayor of Brady, Texas, and vice-president of the Brady Aviation Company. From 1959 until his death 11 years later he was president of Texas A & M (Agricultural & Mechanical) University. President Lyndon Johnson awarded Rudder the Distinguished Service Medal (DSM) in 1967.

William O. Darby, the man who founded the lst Ranger Battalion, raised three Ranger battalions in all, saw action in North Africa, Sicily and Italy, and he was awarded DSC, DSM, Silver Star, Oak Leaf cluster to the Purple Heart. He was killed by a shell fragment when serving on the staff of the 10th Mountain Division in northern Italy with the end of the war just a week away. He was posthumously promoted to Brigadier-General. Darby had earlier sent a message to the officers and men of the 1st, 3rd and 4th Ranger Battalions, all deactivated at Camp Butner, North Carolina on 26 October 1944.

He wrote with pride of having served with them and said "We the living Rangers will never forget our fallen comrades. They and the ideals for which they fought will remain ever present among us …No better way can I sum up my feelings of pride for your splendid achievements than to state this: Commanding the Rangers was like driving a team of very high spirited horses. No effort was needed to get them to go forward. The problem was to hold them in check".

Len Lomell received the Distinguished Service Cross and Jack Kuhn the Silver Star for their actions on Pointe du Hoc. Lomell was wounded three times and received a battlefield commission before the war was over. He established a successful law practice in New Jersey.

Unbelievably, Kuhn made it to V-E Day without a scratch and ended the war as a 1st Sergeant. Serving in the United States Marine Corps in the Korean War, later Kuhn worked as a police officer and worked his way up through the ranks to become chief of the Altoona Police Department.

In various forms, Rangers have served since in Korea and Vietnam, after which the US Army realised that it lacked special forces which could be moved at speed - and so two battalions of the 75th Infantry (Rangers) were raised in 1974. Since then a number of campaigns have involved Rangers and in 1984 a third battalion

ABOVE: Rangers bringing German prisoners to an assembly point on the east side of Pointe du Hoc. The Pointe is at the right in the background. *(USN)*

ABOVE: The same location as it is today. *(AN)*

was formed, as was a regimental headquarters at Fort Benning, Georgia. It is still there. Some Rangers took part in Desert Storm (1993) and then in the controversial and costly events in Somalia in 1993. Since 9/11 the Rangers have been kept busy - and suffered casualties.

Since 1946, the British commando role has been entirely the preserve of the Corps of Royal Marines. In World War Two, particularly in view of the requirement for amphibious capability, some experts wondered why RM and RN senior officers allowed the Army to gain the initiative in 1940. Julian Thompson, who led No. 3 Commando Brigade in the Falklands War of 1982, retired as a Major-General and is now a military historian, believes much of this was due to the fault of the Royal Navy and its officers.

The Royal Marines had a division earmarked for operations that did not materialise in World War Two and this kept its brigades from being utilised on raids as originally envisaged. One RM staff officer believed that Marines should not be 'turned over to the Army as happened in the First World War' but as Thompson argued in his *The Royal Marines. From Sea Soldiers to a Special Force* it was only when the Marines 'became involved alongside, or in conjunction with, the Army on the main point of effort, in the principal theatres of war, that the years of frustration and waste for the Corps ended'. Thompson also claims: '...the

most suitable employment for fighting men is marching towards the sound of the guns, not picking and choosing where they will fight'.

At the end of the war, the British Army commandos numbered from 1-9, then - missing out 10 (a unit formed of numerous trained Allied commandos who tended to be used piecemeal attached to other formations) - 11 and 12. RM Commandos numbered 40-48, and three are still in being in 3 Commando Brigade: nos. 40, 42 and 45.

Controversy still surrounds the use of special or elite forces. By their very nature, they need to be more intensively trained than what might be termed standard infantry. In action, their very 'lightness' means that faced with large conventional opposition they can enjoy initial success, but very soon have to rely on

others to follow up quickly with heavy-weapon support and supplies. Increasing the size of special units also raises a valid question: at what point does 'elite' cease to be just that and become standard? In the battle for Huertgen Forest, Rudder had complained to some senior staff officers about the 'misuse' of his 2nd Ranger Battalion. It did not work and in a battle for Bergstein, his unit lost over half its strength, most lost in the cause of defending a hill.

Looking back to Pointe du Hoc, some argue that the position could have been assaulted from landward, after a successful landing at Omaha. Leaving the horror of Omaha alive and being battle ready was no easy matter, as the world now knows. And in the meantime the 155mm guns could have inflicted further real damage on Utah and Omaha beaches. What about a paratroop

ABOVE: Rangers at the top of the cliff face at Pointe du Hoc engaging the enemy. *(USN)*

ABOVE: The same location as it is today. *(AN)*

assault ? Not if the chaotic results of the D-Day air drops by 82nd and 101st Airborne divisions are any guide. Then, of course, the Germans expected any attack on Pointe du Hoc to come from any point - except up the cliff face!

In 1984, on the 40th anniversary of the landings, the then President of the United States, Ronald Reagan, addressed the survivors of the Ranger's assault, gathered in front of the impressive memorial to their feats. "Forty summers have passed since the battle that you fought here. You were young the day you took these cliffs; some of you were hardly more than boys, with the deepest joys of life before you. Yet you risked everything here. Why? Why did you do it? What impelled you to put aside the instinct for self-preservation and risk your lives to take these cliffs? What inspired all the men of

the armies that met here? We look at you, and somehow we know the answer. It was faith, and belief; it was loyalty and love.

"The men of Normandy had faith that what they were doing was right, faith that they fought for all humanity, faith that a just God would grant them mercy on this beachhead or on the next. It was the deep knowledge - and pray God we have not lost it - that there is a profound moral difference between the use of force for liberation and the use of force for conquest. You were here to liberate, not to conquer, and so you and those others did not doubt your cause. And you were right not to doubt".

James Earl Rudder did not doubt. Yet he cannot be blamed for wondering 10 years after just how he and his men managed their astonishing triumph at Pointe du Hoc.

By 09.00 hours on 6 June 1944 Rudder and his men had captured the gun battery and destroyed the 155mm guns. (AN)